About Time

About Time

Inventing the Fourth Dimension

William Friedman

A Bradford Book
The MIT Press
Cambridge, Massachusetts
London, England

This book was typeset in Palatino by Compset, Inc. and printed and bound in the United States of America.

Library of Congress Cataloging-in-Publication Data

Friedman, William J.
  About time : inventing the fourth dimension / William Friedman.
    p.   cm.
  "A Bradford book." $19.95
  Includes bibliographical references.
  ISBN 0-262-06133-3
  1. Time perception. 2. Space and time. I. Title.
  BF468.F75   1990
  153.7'53—dc20   90-30771
                                           CIP

60470

To my parents, Philip and Serene

Contents

Preface

In the 1847 edition of *The Pickwick Papers,* Dickens observed that "prefaces, though seldom read, are continually written." I write this preface at the suggestion of a respected colleague who told me that he likes to find out about the background of an author's interest and why a book was put together as it was. I am reassured by the fact that Dickens went on to ignore his own advice.

My involvement in the topic of time dates to the first weeks of graduate school, when I arrived with a general interest in cognitive development, but no well-defined specialization. In a meeting with my advisor, Michael Davidson, I happened to mention a vague idea that we seem to understand time by spatializing it. (The idea is an old one in philosophy, but I didn't know it at the time.) I noticed that the topic seemed to engage his attention, and, graduate students being a little insecure about their own ideas, this must have had a strong impact on me. Over the succeeding years of graduate school, with a mix of freedom and encouragement for which I will always be grateful, I conducted experiments that dealt with children's representation of time and space—some successful, others not. But along the way I learned that I enjoyed the process of turning vague questions into specific experiments whose results provide at least partial answers. I also discovered, as young scholars so often do, the pleasures of delving deeply into a single topic and finding successive layers of interesting questions.

I sometimes think about people's career choices in the language of learning theory, according to which behaviors, like a rat's lever presses, can be reinforced or extinguished. Over the years my interests in time have been reinforced by the fun of finding one question after another to ponder and colleagues and students willing to share the work on some mutually interesting problem. At long intervals, but of reinforcement value far out of proportion to their number, have been a series of stimulating meetings with other researchers who are fascinated by the psychology of time.

I wrote this book because I wanted to make these issues and ideas available to a wider group than the few specialists. I suspect that most people have wondered at some point about the nature of time; certainly there has been considerable interest in recent books on time in the universe, geologists' conceptions of time, the history of clock technology, and the sociology of time. If I am right, there may be interest too in the most intimate of time's many facets—the nature of temporal experience.

This book was written with the general educated reader in mind, but, I now realize, always with an image of my colleagues looking over my shoulder. Because I spend much of my life teaching undergraduates, I have reason to believe that issues and findings in psychology, and even the way psychologists think about problems, are accessible to people with a wide range of intellectual interests. For the minority of readers who are students and other researchers, I have included information about my sources, but for the general reader have moved the scholarly paraphernalia and elaborations to the end of the book and attempted to err, if anything, on the side of brevity. For those specialists on the psychology of time who are the phantoms over my shoulder, I have tried to provide some fresh perspectives on the issues that we study, fully recognizing the myopia, and possible quirkiness, of any one such view.

This is an occasion to thank the people who have contributed to this book and collaborated with me on studies, some of which are mentioned in the following chapters. My collaborators include Pamela Blewitt, Arnold Wilkins, Susan Brudos, and Frank Laycock, and the many wonderful students who have served as research assistants. I would especially like to thank those who were kind enough to read and provide comments on my writing: Frank Laycock, Françoise Macar, Mark Friedman, Ascher Koriat, Douglas Poynter, and Friedrich Wilkening. I have benefited from stimulating conversations during my sabbaticals at the Applied Psychology Unit in Cambridge, England, and at the University of Grenoble, and I am indebted to Oberlin College for providing the leave time for me to complete this work and to the Psychology Institute, Stockholm University, for making their facilities available to me. Finally, I would like to thank my wife Britt and son Joshua, who were understanding enough that the book was eventually written, but sensible enough that we did end up bicycling, skiing, or going for a walk when that was the right thing to do with the time.

About Time

Chapter 1

Introduction

A Collection of Temporal Experiences

All of us have a haphazard collection of impressions of time, stored away like the contents of an attic against the unlikely event that they will ever be used. We sometimes come across them, stimulating a brief sense of familiarity, before they are stowed away again and forgotten. We recognize the particular feeling when a wait in traffic seems endless or an evening spent with friends rushes by as if a piece of time had dropped away. We notice the experience of temporal disorientation on holidays and each spring and fall are a bit confused by the shift to or from daylight saving time. Our attention is called to time when we encounter disparate attitudes in people of two cultures, as when an American traveler, who feels impelled to rush through the meal and on to the next site, is served by a French waiter, who is trying to provide a gracious and leisurely repast. Usually, however, time remains in the background. It seems to surround us like space and is just as likely to be unnoticed. With little attention we move about in space without bumping into things, and so we seldom bump into time.

But if we were to haul out our collection of temporal experiences, dust them off, and sort them like the contents of an attic arrayed on the lawn, we might actually find some striking consistencies in what seems at first a stray assortment. This urge to order things, to compartmentalize an unruly mass, is a common starting point of scientific inquiry, and it is a fitting place to begin an inquiry into the human experience of time.

One pile in anyone's classification would include impressions of time passing at variable rates. Over the last several centuries clockmakers have struggled to make time a uniform dimension, transforming a technology of sandglasses into one of atomic clocks, accurate to one part in ten billion. But our raw experience of time stubbornly resists their advances. Alongside the world of clocks is another anomalous world, partially captured by our metaphors of time flying by or inching along, in which activities and moods more than the rhythms of nature modulate the pace. We have a vivid and changing sense of the rate at which the present is moving by us and of lengths of intervals in our recent past. If one collects a sufficient number of these experiences of the uneven flow of time, it is hard to help but wonder how we come by our impressions of quantities of time. Is there some sort of mental clock, less perfect than those that the clockmakers have fashioned, that speeds up and slows down?

Another set of temporal experiences concerns our sense of the past. Memories are as real and meaningful to us as any feelings of time passing in the present, and the vast majority of our memories seem to belong to a place in time. Many times a day we try to localize past events in time, in effect writing our own history, as we recall when we took a particular vacation, when we watered the plants, when we last wrote to a friend. Perhaps we are most struck by this sense of past time when the normal fading of impressions with time is violated and an event we know to have occurred long ago seems "like yesterday." Although it appears perfectly obvious that we should have a chronological past, it is by no means clear what information we use to figure the chronology. Is the mind a kind of archives, ordered or indexed by date? Do we actually use the fading of memories to tell what events belong to yesterday and what to our distant childhood?

In addition to our sense of a past and our impressions of the rate of time's passage, we also encounter on a daily basis a more autonomous, impersonal time—the time of the clock and calendar. Though external and separable from subjective time, our lives are so thoroughly interwoven with these time systems that the systems in fact form an intimate part of our temporal experience. The day, month, and year, and even the artificial hour and week, have been internalized as natural units for dividing and structuring the past, present, and future. Many people report having internalized the calendar system in the form of personal images, with their lives progressing on mental circles of the months or rows of days of the week. Others complain that digital watch displays are dissonant with their own tendency to think of clock intervals in terms of space. Whatever the nature of our representations, it is clear that an important part of the experience of time involves building mental models of recurrent temporal patterns in our environment.

A fourth class of time experiences stems from an irresistible tendency to believe in a present. Most of us find quite startling the claim of some physicists and philosophers that the present has no special status in the physical world, that there is only a sequence of times, that the past, present, and future are only distinguishable in human consciousness. In our experiential world there is a sharp contrast between memories of the past and plans for the future, and much of our temporal thinking is devoted to determining the current time (1:00, Wednesday, April . . .) and considering the relative times of past and future events. The rare occasions when we are disoriented—when we come out of movies, when it is a holiday or we are on vacation, when we wake from sleep—show how much a sense of temporal orientation is part of our normal experience. Like our sense of a chronological past, this sense of a place in time seems mundane, but is in fact quite a mysterious affair. How is it that we are able to constantly rebuild the present?

Our collection of temporal experiences must also include encounters with people who appear to have different views of time. None of these are more likely to highlight what we take for granted about time than our conversations with children. Parents notice that their deeply internalized world of clocks and calendars is quite alien to young children. Youngsters talk about the times and durations of event with wild disregard for our conventions: "yesterday" is any time in the past and "tomorrow" any time in the future, a short wait is "five hours," and one's favorite television show comes on at "44 o'clock." Even more fundamental questions about our view of time are raised when we consider the temporal experience of young infants, who have had little exposure to a temporally ordered environment and who might even lack a sense that events follow one another in a sequence. We also come across apparent personality differences in adults' attitudes toward time. A wait on a train platform, even of the most reliable of railroads, will show some people pacing and repeatedly checking their watches while others sit patiently. Travelers find variation in temporal attitudes too, as people of different cultures show divergent beliefs about the importance of punctuality and the efficient use of time.

Clearly there are meaningful clusters in our collection of temporal experiences: variations in the flow of subjective time, a sense of a chronological past, mental models of recurrent time patterns, an ever-changing vantage point, and encounters with people who hold different views of time. It is also clear that no sooner do we begin to sort the experiences than we find that the categories come laden with questions, just as the piles of objects from an attic invite us to ask, "What were these used for?" or "How were they made?" Our impressions of the rate of time's flow must be the surface manifestation of some deeper processes. Do these involve an internal clock? How then can we explain the distortions that occur with such regularity? Our sense of an ordered past, as we saw, raises questions about how we know the time of past events and in what sense they occupy a place in time. The fact that we must carry around with us mental models of time patterns is cause to wonder about the nature of these representations. How do people think about time patterns? In images? In words? Even if we were to know what the representations were like, how could they account for our fourth category of experiences, those surrounding our ability to know our place in time? How can our present position within the patterns by updated? The peculiarities of children's view of time provoke questions about the origins and development of temporal knowledge, and, like the cultural and personality differences we notice, about how different the temporal experience of other people really is. These are the sorts of questions that intrigue students of the psychology of time, and they are the questions that concern us in the remainder of this book.

When questions are raised about the nature of time, as they have been throughout history, many different sorts of answers can be given. Cosmologists can tell us about the evolution of the universe, geologists about the history of the earth, biologists about the organic processes underlying temporal adaptation in living things, and historians about the development and spread of clocks. Even our narrower range of questions about the nature of humans' experience of time have been addressed by philosophers and students of the humanities as well as psychologists. What then is special about psychological inquiry, the line that we pursue in this book?

Psychologists share with many philosophers and scholars in the humanities a fascination with human experience, but we suffer from a certain impatience that compels us to conduct experiments. Over the last century thousands of articles have been published on the psychology of time, most of them reporting one or more experiments. Psychological experiments are systematic observations of behavior, usually under conditions carefully controlled by the experimenter. In the area of time we mainly ask the subjects in our experiments to assess temporal intervals, to remember the time of past events, or to reason about time systems, always controlling some variables we think will help reveal the nature of the underlying processes. The use of experimental control can be a powerful tool and is undoubtedly responsible for many of the successes of the natural sciences. But operationalizing, measuring, and controlling can sometimes lead to distorting or trivializing the phenomenon under study. It is essential to understand the types of evidence that are used to support one or another view of the nature of temporal experience, so that one can decide for oneself how persuasive this evidence is. Furthermore, when the basic evidence is available, readers can evaluate some of their own ideas about the experience of time. For these reasons I have resisted the temptation to simply give conclusions, and the following chapters contain many descriptions of experiments.

Another feature of psychological inquiry, particularly in the specialty of cognitive psychology, is the tendency to consider a number of possible models of the phenomenon of interest and to use experiments to choose among them. The models are ways of describing mental processes and often rely on analogies to something more tangible than the mind itself (for example, terms like *searching*, *scanning*, and *accessing* are frequently used). Fortunately, like the experiments themselves, the models are usually easy to explain, so even people who are not cognitive psychologists can get a good feel for the kinds of explanations they favor. For many of the phenomena to be considered, including time perception, memory, and orientation, we mimic this approach of trying out the competing models.

Psychological models are not the products of divine revelation but are thought up by real people and are therefore pregnant with their assumptions. Similarly any book is built around a set of assumptions about its topic. The author's views inevitably influence the selection of topics and the way in which questions are posed, as well as, more obviously, the framing of conclusions. This book reflects a particular view of the psychology of time, a view that is best made explicit at the outset.

Much of the history of the philosophy of time is a series of attempts to find time's essence, whether in nature or in consciousness. Among those conceptions tying time to the physical world, time has been defined as motions, as the succession of events, and as an absolute, universal framework. Mentalist definitions refer to the perception of succession and simultaneity or the succession of ideas in consciousness. In the midst of all this diversity is a common tendency to treat time as a single thing. Psychologists too seem inclined to seek a single entity, as they write of "the concept," "the notion," or "the sense" of time. Perhaps the fact that we have a single word for time has seduced us into searching for its essence.

However, at least from a psychological point of view, it seems far more productive to consider the many things that time is in the world and the many ways in which humans experience it. Our environment is rich in temporal structures—in music, in language, in the characteristic durations of familiar events, and in the recurrent cycles of nature and our own activities. To define time as some unitary dimension that cuts across all of these features is to lose sight of the special challenges they pose for perception and cognition. We rely on our ears and specialized regions of the brain to perform the elementary analysis of language and music, but such mechanisms cannot explain our ability to estimate how long the coffee has been perking or to judge the order of past events in our lives. An even clearer demonstration of the multiplicity of time in the world and in the mind comes from the study of child development. As we will see in chapter 6, children respond to the temporal patterning of stimuli and sequence their own actions well before they acquire a mature sense of time measurement or grasp the workings of the calendar. The many separate aspects of time that children come to understand in the course of development and the gradual nature of this development show us how deceptive it is to speak of "the notion of time." The division of this book into chapters on perception, memory, representation, orientation, development, and individual and group differences—along the lines of the sorting scheme described above—is based on a belief that we are more likely to understand the nature of temporal experience by examining its different facets than by searching for a common core.

In addition to a strong disinclination to seek a single essence of time or time experience, I approach the psychology of time with another bias: A large proportion of the thousands of studies in this area concern what is called the perception of time. These are the sorts of studies described in chapter 2; they involve judgments of the length of brief intervals, usually several minutes or less. As we will see, this research is helpful in answering questions about the processes underlying our experience of the rate of time's passage. But as significant as these questions are, I believe that research on time perception has received much too large a share of the attention devoted to the psychology of time and that not enough attention has been spent exploring the rich possibilities offered by cognitive and developmental psychology. The dominance of time perception research is probably a consequence of a particular view of the psychology of time, one that I do not share, that time perception is the foundation of temporal experience. In this view our knowledge of time is rooted in the perception of moment-to-moment changes in our environment or consciousness of internal, clocklike processes. We learn to recognize the feel of particular intervals—seconds, minutes—and these become the building blocks of our knowledge of longer intervals of time.

This attempt to derive the experience of time from the perception of brief intervals seems to me like trying to explain human's knowledge of space by the laws of visual perception. We come to understand the layout of a town or city by piecing together information learned from many different journeys, from directions others have given us, and from maps, eventually forming mental representations of large-scale spaces (often called *cognitive maps*) that are much more powerful than any collection of snapshot views. Similarly our knowledge of time goes far beyond the piecing together of impressions of brief durations. Of course the brain receives information successively over time. But, to an extent unique among species, we are gifted with mental processes that allow us to step outside the "now," the endless succession of stimuli, and to build elaborate models of time: of the fluctuations of nature, the past, present, and future, near time and far time, even the fictitious time of novels and plays. Some of these models are built up in the course of development as children learn about the time patterns around them and the conventional systems adults use to partition time. But time is also constructed and reconstructed many times a day as part of our recurrent attempts to localize memories in the past, plan future activities, and understand our current place in time. When seen from this point of view, the challenge to a psychology of time becomes one of understanding the numerous mental processes that underlie our construction of temporal experience.

Sorting through one's attic often has mixed success, as may be true of our inquiry about time as well. We begin with the aim of tidying and organizing but usually end up with the afternoon gone and our attic far from orderly, as we become lost in examining and contemplating its contents. The following chapters show that we are far from having a tidy picture of the mental processes underlying the human experience of time. But there is a certain fascination just in poring over one's collection and the promise that some of the objects will never again seem the same.

Chapter 2

Perception

The Mind's Timekeepers

The act of reading a watch is seldom the mechanical registration of information. Look at your watch and you are likely to be surprised at how time has flown or inched along since you checked it last, or you may congratulate yourself for your success in guessing the time to within a few minutes. Clearly we have distinct impressions about quantities of time, impressions that are quite separate from its formal measurement. These impressions are what we mean when we talk about time perception.

As commonplace as time perception is, it must surely be among the most enigmatic of human abilities. On the one hand we do show remarkable precision in estimating the amount of time that has passed on at least some occasions. On the other hand our impressions of duration are often buffeted by the currents of experiences like boredom, anticipation, and absorption. This mixture of precision and distortion leads to the two central questions of this chapter: Is there really a "sense" of time? and Why does the passage of time seem uneven? These questions have been pursued by psychologists for more than a century and have stimulated the vast majority of research on the psychology of time.

The large quantity of research on time perception is no doubt partly due to the ease of measurement—all you need is a clock. The subjects in your experiments can indicate their impressions of time by verbally estimating the length[1] of some duration you present, they can press a button for some amount of time you specify, or they can attempt to reproduce some duration that you model for them. The real challenges in studying time perception are the development of precise ideas about the mechanisms involved and the design of experiments to test them. As we will see, two general sorts of explanations for human time perception have been offered, and they have been evaluated in the light of numerous types of evidence: The first kind of explanation is rooted in specific physiological processes. The second appeals to general cognitive processes such as noticing changes in our environment and remembering or failing to remember events.

Is There a "Sense" of Time?

When we talk about a *sense* of time, it is important that we be clear about whether we are using the term literally or metaphorically. In common usage one can refer to a sense of self, a sense of purpose, or even a sense of foreboding. But in its narrower usage the term connotes sensation, the neural coding of physical stimuli impinging on the body. We have senses of vision, of hearing, of smell, taste, and so forth, each depending on specific neurons that transduce energy or chemical stimuli and on specific pathways leading to the brain. Time, of course, is not a physical or chemical stimulus to which neural structures can respond. There is no environmental time that can excite a time sense, only the physical events that we consider as contained in time.

To be sure, some environmental events carry information about time. The position of the sun and social activities around us serve to tell us where we are within a day. But when we think of time perception or a time sense, we tend to mean a direct impression of some duration rather than inference from cues to the present time.

If there is a time sense, it must be built on some internal process that changes over time. In principle our time sense could be the counting of heartbeats, breaths, one of the many cycles of brain electrical activity, or any other repetitive physiological event. There are many *possible* bases of human time perception, but is there any evidence for the existence for such a biological clock? In fact there is overwhelming support for internal processes that keep track of the time within the daily cycle. These *circadian clocks*[2] (from the Latin meaning "approximately a day") are remarkable adaptations to the 24-hour cycles of light and temperature, but their involvement in human time perception remains uncertain.

Circadian Clocks

Circadian time keeping is characteristic of nearly all living things, from single-celled organisms to humans. By simulating the 24-hour cycle internally, organisms are able to anticipate external cyclic changes, such as the availability of food, the presence of predators, or the coming of dawn. Circadian clocks allow animals to marshal and conserve energy supplies to best exploit their fluctuating environment. In some cases there is even a competitive advantage to being the first to arrive at a food source at a particular time each day. Many flower species are so regular in their daily opening times that the Swedish botanist Carl Linnaeus was able to plant a flower clock, with different species blooming at each hour during the day. Bees are adept at learning to link odors, colors, and locations to particular times within their circadian cycles, an apparent adaptation to the regularity of their floral food sources.

Circadian timing is involved in the regulation of numerous behavioral and physiological rhythms.[3] Sleep-wake cycles, feeding cycles, body temperature cycles, and a variety of hormonal and metabolic oscillations are all under the control of circadian clocks. There are even regular daily fluctuations in human cognitive and motor performance. (For example, the time required to respond to the onset of lights or sounds is, on average, greatest at about 4:00 AM, and performance on mental arithmetic tasks also typically reaches a low during the early morning hours.) In seasonally breeding mammals circadian systems determine the time of year by sensing whether dawn and dusk come relatively early or late according to the internal clock, triggering hormonal and behavioral changes essential to mating.

The concept of circadian clocks is necessary not because an animal's behavior is periodic over a day—the animal might simply respond to time-of-day cues like the temperature or the position of the sun—but because they are relatively independent of the environment. Like any good clock they run for some useful period of time without having to be reset. Many studies with plants and animals have shown that circadian cycles persist even when the organism is deprived of all possible external time cues. For example, in a number of experiments[4] humans have lived for many weeks in caves or other underground chambers where constant light, temperature, and sound conditions prevailed. The results show a striking persistence of near-24-hour cycles (usually closer to 25 hours), especially in body temperature, over periods as long as many weeks. Actually the relative independence of circadian rhythms is patently obvious to anyone who has flown across many time zones. One's physiology seems to have a kind of inertia that for a while makes it oblivious to local time cues.

The independence of circadian clocks is *relative* because under normal conditions environmental cues, such as light changes at dawn and dusk, resynchronize the clocks with the earth's rotation. Although light is especially important in most species, certain other periodic cues can help to keep the clocks in phase. For example, most blind people respond to the same circadian rhythms as sighted people, presumably because social cycles convey sufficient time-of-day information.

Circadian clocks seem to be specialized for time tracking on a relatively long time scale. But might they also be responsible for time measurement on the shorter scales that we usually think of when considering the perception of time? Might circadian clocks be the basis of a time sense? Unfortunately there is no direct evidence that allows us to answer the question. Several considerations seem to weigh against the involvement of circadian clocks in time perception, but there are also some findings that seem to link the two.

One reason to doubt the involvement of circadian clocks is that they do not appear to be precise enough to account for time perception abilities. Humans can easily discriminate temporal intervals that differ by only a few seconds or less, but the circadian clock shows errors on the order of many minutes per day.[5] This would seem to make the task of time perception a bit like trying to time a short sprint with the minute hand of a watch. However, this argument is not conclusive because, at least in principle, the mechanism underlying time perception could involve the counting of the "ticks" that drive the circadian clock, not reading the dial itself. Because circadian clocks appear to be accurate to the order of a few percent per day or less, similarly accurate short-term oscillations (if they are involved in such clocks) might be more than adequate to account for our accuracy in judging brief intervals.

A second argument against the circadian clock explanation is that certain influences appear to distort time perception, but not the functioning of the clocks. For example, there is at least some evidence (considered in detail later) that humans shorten or lengthen their duration estimates with increases or decreases in body temperature. An important and well-established feature of circadian clocks, however, is their relative constancy despite temperature changes. Similarly protein ingestion shortens the production of a well-learned time interval in rats,[6] but it is very unlikely that variations in eating and fasting have a similar effect on the rate of the circadian clock.

In opposition to these arguments there is some intriguing, though still limited, evidence linking time judgments to circadian cycles. In several of the studies in which humans have lived in temporal isolation for many weeks, they have been asked to judge different intervals of time. These judgments have been compared with the subjects' circadian rhythms and of course with the objective passage of time. In about one-third of these cases, as the isolation period continued, the sleep-wake cycle uncoupled from its normal 24-hour period and lengthened substantially, with very long sleep and very long waking periods. When this occurred, duration judgments were sometimes affected. One subject who was asked to signal the beginning and end of periods ranging from 30 seconds to two minutes produced intervals that were about double the objective length by the end of his stay.[7] In another study[8] subjects were instructed to press a button at what they believed to be one-hour intervals. Actual productions were longer the greater the length of the subject's sleep-wake cycle: Those subjects with very long days also marked off very long hours. These correlations between time judgments and the sleep-wake cycle raise the possibility that both are products of a common internal clock. However, before this interpretation can be accepted, more research showing a consistent relationship between circadian cycle length and subjective duration is needed.[9]

Circadian clocks are not the only biological mechanisms on which time perception might rest, so the case for a sense of time does not stand or fall on this evidence. In fact most advocates of biological explanations have assumed that some other periodic physiological process produces the "ticks" of the perceptual clock. There is a surprising variety in these explanations and the evidence relevant to them.

Other Internal Timers
The ideal evidence for the existence of a time sense would be the demonstration of a physiological rhythm whose rate is consistently correlated with the lengthening or shortening of time judgments. But no one has yet identified such a rhythm. Many candidates have been tested, including heart rate, respiration, and the alpha rhythm recorded from scalp electrodes, but none seems to be the perceptual clock. The failure to find a base time rhythm, though, does not mean that such a clock does not exist, any more than the long search for the physiological substrate of circadian clocks has cast doubt on their existence.[10] In most biological theories of time perception, the internal clock is a hypothetical entity whose properties are studied by indirect means.

A common feature of all biological clock theories[11] is the presence of some oscillatory process, analogous to the swings of a clock's pendulum, whose cycles can be counted by some other mechanism. There are many variations in how such a system might work, but in all of the models, changes in the rate of oscillation will produce regular changes in time judgments. The specific relation between oscillation rate and time judgments is sometimes a bit confusing (even for experts), so it is worth spelling out rather precisely.

Imagine that someone's oscillator is running too fast for some reason.[12] If they are asked to press a button for what they believe to be 10 seconds (using the method called production), the interval they produce should be shorter than usual. By analogy a metronome set at too high a speed would reach the end of a measure in too short a time. Alternatively we could use the method of estimation: presenting a standard interval, say, one of 10 seconds, and asking the person to judge how long it seemed to be. A fast-running oscillator should lead them to give a longer estimate than they normally would (say, 15 seconds instead of about 10). To use the same analogy, more metronome beats would have passed during the interval than at the normal setting. Finally, one could say that people with a fast-running oscillator experience clock time—the amount of time it takes for a minute or an hour to elapse—as passing slower than it usually does. (The music they listen to seems too slow in comparison with their metronome.) All of these effects of course would be reversed in the case of an oscillator that was running too slow: unusually long productions, short estimates of intervals, and clock time appearing to pass too rapidly. These sorts of predictions lead to two of the main types of evidence for biological clock theories—studies of the effects of body temperature and drugs on time judgments.[13]

One of the earliest observations of the effect of body temperature on time perception was made by the physiologist Hudson Hoagland[14] during the 1930s, when his wife was ill with influenza. Hoagland made a 20-minute trip to the drugstore and returned to find that his wife, whose temperature was 104°F, believed he had been gone for a much longer time. Suspecting that this time distortion might be due to some physiological process related to body temperature, Hoagland asked his wife to make a series of judgments of 60 seconds, counting at the rate of one per second, at various times during her illness. He found that his wife's counting rate was greater (that is, she produced 60 seconds in a shorter time) when her temperature was higher. Because chemical reactions and many biological processes take place more rapidly at higher temperatures, Hoagland hypothesized that the time sense depends on a temperature-sensitive chemical clock in the brain.

In the decades since Hoagland's proposal, a series of experiments have tested the relation between body temperature and time judgments.[15] These have not been the most pleasant of experiments for subjects! The variety of interventions used to raise or lower body temperature have included passing high-frequency alternating currents through the body, having subjects work in 124°F rooms until near collapse, and staying lightly clothed in a 32°F room to the point of violent shivering.

Unfortunately, despite all of the discomfort involved, this research has not produced an entirely consistent picture. A number of these studies have found the expected relation between body temperature and time estimates. For example, a British researcher, Alan Baddeley, collected temperature readings and time estimates from a group of divers before and after they dove into 39°F sea water off the coast of Wales. From before to after the dives, their average oral temperature dropped from 97.39° to 95.03°F, and the time taken to count out a subjective 60 seconds increased from about 64 seconds to about 70 seconds. This is just what we would expect if the internal clock were ticking at a slower rate. On the other hand not all studies have confirmed Hoagland's prediction, nor has a continuous relation between body temperature level and amount of distortion always been found.

Another problem for Hoagland's biological clock hypothesis is that temperature changes could exert their influence on time perception by speeding or slowing the succession of mental states rather than by affecting the oscillation rate of a physiological time base. For example, if higher temperatures were to bring about a flood of sensations and thoughts, we might be led to overestimate some interval, assuming that the registration of changes is the basis of time perception. Notice, however, that we cannot interpret the temperature effects simply by referring to the commonsense observation that time passes slowly when we are uncomfortable (for example, sitting on a hot stove). This is because most of the studies in which body temperature is lowered, even to a very unpleasant extent, have shown that external time appears to pass relatively rapidly.

A second, related argument for the biological clock theories is the influence of drugs on time perception. Users of psychoactive substances often report striking alterations in the rate at which time appears to pass, and some of these effects have been confirmed in controlled studies. For example, it has been shown that LSD[16] and THC[17] (the active constituent of marijuana) both lead to exaggerated estimates of intervals of clock time or unusually short productions when subjects are asked to mark off a specified quantity of time (as if an internal clock was running too fast). Amphetamines have similar effects,[18] whereas tranquilizers,[19] alcohol,[20] and anesthetics[21] lead to underestimates or overproductions (as if an internal clock was running too slow). These drug-induced time distortions have sometimes been interpreted in terms of alterations of a physiological pacemaker. In one view a metabolically related clock, of the sort posited by Hoagland, is sped or slowed by drugs that raise or lower body temperature.[22] Another explanation of at least some of the drug effects is that the oscillator rate varies according to prevailing levels of the neurotransmitter dopamine.[23] Drugs that raise the levels of dopamine are thought to speed the oscillator and those that lower dopamine levels to slow it.

The temperature account of the drug effects is a bit troublesome because most of these drugs produce quite small effects on body temperature[24] and because THC does not fit the pattern—it lowers body temperature, but leads to shorter productions.[25] It is also by no means clear whether the dopamine hypothesis could explain all or just some of the drug effects. Perhaps a more fundamental problem with this kind of evidence for a biological clock is that drugs invariably produce a multitude of physiological alterations in the brain. This makes it difficult to pin their effects on one kind of mechanism or another. A special biological pacemaker may be responsible, or the drugs may influence time perception by affecting other cognitive processes. For example, some researchers[26] have attributed drug-induced time distortions to the inward focus or lack of concentration that these substances can produce. If a drug brings about a cascade of experiences on the one hand or a sparse series of impressions on the other, we might easily be led to misjudge how much time has really elapsed. Thus we see that drug effects, like body temperature effects, do not commit us to any particular explanation of time perception, such as one relying on a physiological clock.

Actually what is probably the most persuasive evidence for a biologically based time sense comes from a completely different kind of evidence—the ability of animals to judge intervals of time. We have already seen that circadian timing—measurement of approximately 24-hour intervals—is possible in animals other than humans. But in recent years there have been a number of important demonstrations of animals' ability to learn temporal intervals on the order of seconds and minutes and some provocative ideas about the adaptive value of such abilities. For our purposes these findings are significant because, if there is a true time "sense," it is unlikely to be unique to humans. Vision, hearing, touch, and our other sensory modalities are all shared with other animal species (though of course there are differences from species to species in the particulars of each sensory system).

The ability of laboratory animals to measure time has been known since Ivan Pavlov's pioneering work on the conditioning of physiological responses, but most research is based on methods developed in the 1930s by the learning theorist B. F. Skinner.[27] Skinner had been using his standard technique for teaching new behaviors to rats, reinforcing them with food pellets each time they produced some desired behavior, such as pressing a lever. In an effort to conserve his food supplies, he tried a new schedule (called the fixed-interval schedule), rewarding behaviors only once per minute. Skinner found a resulting pattern that has since been demonstrated in a wide variety of species:

the rat would press the lever infrequently at the beginning of the interval after the last reinforcement was available and accelerate the rate of pressing just before one minute elapsed. Because there were no external cues to tell the rat that rewards would soon be available, it must somehow have measured the time interval.

Since Skinner's early work there have been numerous demonstrations of animals' timing abilities using the fixed-interval schedule and other techniques.[28] This research, involving species ranging from goldfish to primates, has shown a number of important properties of animals' timing systems. For example, animals are capable of timing intervals of different lengths. This shows that they do not just possess the equivalent of an egg timer that measures a single duration. Instead their timing system more nearly resembles a stopwatch. There is even evidence that animals can simultaneously time two intervals of different lengths, as if they were capable of running two separate clocks at the same time.[29]

Timing abilities could not have evolved for the amusement of experimental psychologists, so one is left to wonder how they might serve animals in the real world. Some answers have been provided by studies of animal behavior in natural settings. A common problem faced by many species is deciding how long to forage in a given area before giving up and looking for food elsewhere. To illustrate this, imagine that you are hunting for the delicious but rare chanterelle mushrooms in a Swedish forest (as I like to do in the summer). They are difficult to find, so you must usually look very carefully, sometimes brushing aside grass or leaf litter to search. But you might scan a particular patch forever without finding a single chanterelle, so you need some way of knowing when to give up and move on to another area. Elapsed time seems the most reasonable criterion for when to give up. A few seconds is clearly too short a time to spend in a patch if you expect to find many mushrooms, but half an hour is too long. Foraging animals face the same problem, except that for them survival and reproductive success often depend on a careful balancing of energy expended against energy consumed. An ability to measure the amount of time elapsed since food was last found would seem to endow them with a competitive advantage. Consistent with these theoretical considerations, laboratory and field studies[30] have shown that birds seem to take into account the amount of time that has elapsed since they entered the patch or last found food in deciding when to move on.

A particularly striking example of the importance of timing comes from studies of the long-tailed hermit hummingbird,[31] which lives in the jungle of Costa Rica. These birds must obtain nectar from widely spaced flowers whose location is well known to them. The problem is that individual flowers take time to replenish their nectar supplies after a hummingbird has visited them, but if a bird waits too long, a competitor may get there first. This problem is especially acute because of the enormous rate at which hummingbirds burn energy. Clearly a strategy based on rather accurate timing of intervals would bestow a considerable advantage on birds that use it. It is therefore interesting to note that these birds are capable of learning to time their visits to an artificial flower that is experimentally filled 10 minutes after it was last emptied.

All of this evidence seems to provide powerful support for the existence of biologically based mechanisms for timing intervals. Furthermore there are reasons to believe that similar interval timers exist in humans. One is the simple argument that such mechanisms are so pervasive in other species that it is difficult to see why we should lack them. Another is that several studies—using methods similar to those in animal research—have shown that human infants are capable of measuring brief temporal intervals even in the first weeks of life.[32] These findings are important because for young infants, like most of the animal species that have been studied, complex cognitive processes cannot be responsible.

But what role do these biological interval timers play in human time perception? Are our impressions of quantities of time actually based on a time sense? Most of the evidence for the measurement of intervals in animals involves repetitive situations: They gradually learn, over a series of trials, to act once a particular amount of time elapses after some event (a tone, their own last lever press, when food was last obtained . . . .).[33] This sort of learning allows animals to exploit some of the temporal regularities in their world and thereby gain a greater degree of control over their environment. These regularities are recurrent situations in which some response is required at the end of an interval, and it is to the animal's advantage to measure the interval. But there is no evidence that animals have constantly running master clocks that measure the lengths of everything that happens to them.

Similarly humans' biological interval timers are probably used only in circumstances where repetition allows us to build up temporal expectations of the environment. Ironically these interval timers, which must be the products of natural selection, are most evident in our encounters with modern devices like photocopiers, microwave ovens, traffic lights, and coffee machines. Place your coin in the coffee machine, and moments later the cup drops down and fills with coffee. Press the button to make a photocopy, and your finished sheet

Interestingly, simply providing this information, whether before the passage was presented or afterward, led subjects to give shorter estimates of the same 60-second interval. To paraphrase James, familiarity made the experience shrivel up.

The problem with the findings on familiarity and amount remembered is that many studies have failed to show these effects. It may be that James was correct, but that experimenters have not always been successful in manipulating the number or complexity of memories for the stimulus interval. This seems especially likely when one considers that memories for some interval might include not only the stimuli that were presented (for example, the words) but also difficult-to-measure contents like one's thoughts, feelings, and attempts at rehearsal.[50]

A third memory-related phenomenon, which is in fact more reliable than the other two, is that experiences with more distinguishable segments are judged to be longer. For example, a baseball game, with nine innings, might seem longer than a football game, with four quarters, even if the two were of equal duration and were equally interesting. One researcher tested this effect by training three groups of subjects to view the same filmed sequence of modern dance movements as either two, six, or eleven segments.[51] Then all three groups saw the complete 100-second sequence and judged its duration. Those subjects who had been trained on more elements gave longer duration estimates. This finding supports James's observation that ". . . many subdivisions . . . widen the view . . ." of time.

Cognitive Interpretations

We have seen that time perception is indeed malleable and that there are a number of factors that reliably influence our impressions of duration. But our catalog of distortions (see the list) would be far more significant if it could lead us to an understanding of the psychological basis of time perception. The physiological models that we examined previously seem ill equipped to explain most of these illusions (why, for example, would a biological oscillator slow down when more stimuli are presented?), so what alternatives are available to us? Perhaps it is best to start with the fundamental question, If much of time perception is not based on a physiological timer, on what could it rest?

The only possible answers I can imagine involve "quantities" of mental events, perceptions, and memories. If I ask you to estimate the amount of time that you have been reading (relying on impressions alone, not logical cues like the number of pages), what have you to go on but your memory of the psychological and environmental contents of that interval? Or if I tell you in advance that you will be asked to judge the time of a future interval (without counting), what information will you be able to use but the number of mental and external changes?[52] Psychologists, who are constrained by these same basic possibilities, have used a relatively small number of concepts to explain time perception and its distortions.[53] These concepts concern the contents that fill an interval, the influence of attention, and the role of memory.

The contents of an interval can be thought of in part as the number of stimuli that occur within it. This simple notion can explain the second distortion in the list: We gauge duration by assessing the number of events that we have perceived. If more has happened, we conclude that more time has passed. But are time perception and its distortions merely a function of the rate at which events impinge on our senses? This description of an interval's content seems incomplete because it ignores the role of mental events in forming an impression of elapsed time. Even when an interval is relatively empty of external happenings (consider, for example, waiting in a quiet room for a telephone call), we have an impression that it occupies time. In fact the exaggeration of time when we are bored suggests that the density of mental events, such as wondering when the interval will end, can sometimes be a more significant factor than the number of external changes. Also, as we saw previously, certain drug-induced distortions may result from alterations in the flow of mental events. Stimulant and psychedelic drugs obviously do not affect the rate at which things happen in the world, but they may produce exaggerated time estimates by increasing the rate of sensations, ideas, and feelings. For these reasons most explanations of time illusions take into account both external and internal changes. As the Swedish psychologist Marianne Frankenhaeuser put it, "We may assume that the experience of a certain duration is related to the total amount of experience (sensations, perceptions, cognitive and emotional processes, etc.) which takes place within this time period, in short, the *amount of mental content*."[54]

Many of the illusions in the list also seem to involve the role of attention. For example, if the number of external and internal events were the only determinants of time perception, why should absorbing tasks produce underestimates (as they do at least in prospective conditions)? This finding seems particularly paradoxical if we consider that cognitively demanding tasks should induce large numbers of mental events. If you are writing an essay or performing a series of calculations, the great quantity of mental events might be expected to make the duration seem unusually long. The solution to the paradox may be that taxing tasks prevent us from noticing the mental processing we perform in the tasks themselves and perhaps many external events as well.[55] This is clearly a further qualification of the view that amount of mental content determines subjective duration.[56] Apparently some kinds of mental events contribute to the impression of temporal extent and some do not.

The same kind of attentional effect, but in reverse, may be responsible for two of our other distortions. The lengthening of a duration when we know in advance that it is to be judged (distortion 3), or when we are likely to view time as a barrier (distortions 5), may result from greater attention to external and mental content. Thus the watched pot illusion might be explained by our tendency to notice more environmental events (the ticking of the clock, the sound of traffic . . .) and internal changes (wondering if the water is boiling yet, wondering if it is *ever* going to boil . . .).

The distortions listed sixth force us to take memory into account as well. Particularly persuasive are findings that events following the original experience (for example, the information that the passage you just read concerned changing a tire) can shorten time estimates. Such findings cannot be explained by attention or the amount of mental content left at the end of the interval, both of which must have been identical for the group given no cues and the group given the hint about flat tires after the interval. What we remember apparently contributes to our impression of an interval's length.

The distortions listed in this category also suggest that there are several ways of thinking about the "quantities" that might be the basis of remembered time. The crucial quantities could be number of discrete segments (parts to the dance), number of items of information (number of words from the stimulus list), or some aspect of the complexity of the memories (that might distinguish a passage about changing a tire from a sequence of seemingly disconnected sentences about equipment, caution, and lowering the body). But notice that none of these kinds of information is inherently temporal. This fact reveals the fundamental nature of memory-based explanations: Impressions of the length of some past interval of time *derive* from the ordinary contents of memory. It also allows us to understand why such impressions are vulnerable to distortion. With the passage of time and the accumulation of subsequent experiences, information is lost, schematized, reorganized, or embellished. As a consequence impressions of a duration may be stretched or shrunk. Looking back, an important event, such as one's wedding day, may assume exaggerated temporal extent, whereas an insignificant day nearly vanishes in its brevity.

One illusion remains to be explained—the impression that a given interval of calendar time seems briefer as we grow older. This phenomenon has sometimes been attributed to physiological changes that accompany growing older, such as the slowing of metabolic processes.[57] If one accepts a biological clock model, this is a plausible cause because a slower running oscillator should result in the impression that external time is passing faster than it did when we were younger—as the metronome slows, the music appears to speed up. But it is also possible to explain the acceleration in cognitive terms. William James, his philosopher contemporary, Jean-Marie Guyau, and others since[58] have observed that experiences in childhood are varied and distinct, but in adulthood, ". . . each passing year converts some of this experience into automatic routine which we hardly note at all, the days and weeks smooth themselves out in recollection to countless units, and the years grow hollow and collapse." This account appeals to the memory-based explanations that we just discussed: The hollow years seem briefer than early years that conjure vivid and variegated recollections.

We are now in a position to answer the second of our original questions: Why, when we rely on perception alone, does the flow of time seem uneven? The reason is that most of our impressions of "how much" time rest on ordinary mental contents and not on a special time sense. The "quantity" of these contents is subject to the vicissitudes of what occurs, what we notice, and what we remember and thus is vulnerable to distortion. No wonder the act of reading a watch is so often an occasion for surprise.

Chapter 3

Memory

Remembrance of the Times of Things Passed

We all know the experience of thoughts drifting from memory to memory, oblivious to the dominion of time. As I looked out across a rocky beach on an island in Sweden this morning, the crashing waves brought to mind at first the surf at the New Jersey shore when I was a boy and moments later a visit to the beach on which I stood last summer. Our memory seems like a kind of time machine gone haywire, at one moment plummeting backward through the years and at the next reversing itself to bring us back near the present.

But even though the journey is erratic, the memories themselves are not divorced from time. The vast majority of our recollections feel as if they belong to a particular place on our map of the past, even if we cannot always be quite precise, and the déjà vu experience of timeless memory is as infrequent as it is disquieting. No doubt this ability to place memories in time contributes to our sense of identity: We are, in part, our history.

How does time memory work? Is time an automatic, fundamental property of memory, or must we work to localize a memory in time? What psychological processes, at both the time of the original experience and the time of recall, allow us to know when something occurred? Before we look at how psychologists have approached these questions, it is worth trying a few examples of time memory and doing some theorizing of one's own. Consider your answers to the following questions, each of which involves time memory on a different scale: When did you last visit a museum? Which word have you read most recently, *beach* or *theorizing*? Which was more recent, the Chernobyl or Three Mile Island nuclear accident?

In all likelihood your answers to these questions took varying amounts of time, and you probably felt that somewhat different methods were used to reach a solution. The answer to the *beach-theorizing* question, may have appeared to be an immediate and direct process. But remembering and dating your last visit to a museum may have taken more time and involved more mental steps. The

Three Mile Island–Chernobyl question may have struck you as different still if you had a clear sense of their temporal order even without assigning either event a date. Perhaps you would want your theory to explain these seemingly different types of time memory in somewhat different ways. If this is so, you may find yourself sympathetic to more than one of the models that I describe next. These five models are the main ways that psychologists have tried to explain time memory.[1]

Models of Time Memory

The first model is the time-tagging model, and a good metaphor to illustrate it might be a date-stamping machine, used by many offices and libraries to assign a time to new letters or books. Each event is time-tagged as it occurs, and this time information is later recalled along with other aspects of the experience. One theorist proposed that time-tagging is an organic process in which the reading of a biological clock becomes linked to individual events in memory.[2] But it is also possible to imagine a version of the model in which one often notices the time and date when salient events occur, and this temporal information is entered into memory along with other notable aspects, such as *who*, *what*, and *where*.

A second idea is that memory is itself organized sequentially. Rather than assigning dates, the mind simply stores information according to its order of arrival. One proponent of this model has suggested the metaphor of parcels on a moving conveyor belt.[3] Incoming information is bundled together and placed on the belt. As events recede, we are able to gauge their time of occurrence by a kind of distance (or perhaps number of intervening parcels) separating them from the present. This particular version of the time-ordered memory model implies that as events age, it becomes more difficult to determine their precise place in the sequence of experience, just as someone standing at the loading end of the conveyor belt would have trouble judging the order of distant parcels.

The third explanation of time memory is the strength model.[4] This model does not rely on the organization of memory or on time tagging, but instead assumes that memory records, or "traces," change progressively with the passage of time, just as photographs fade when exposed to bright light or radioactive substances decay. If trace strength decreases with time and if we are able to discriminate different strengths, perhaps we judge the time of past events through a kind of carbon dating. Stronger traces are judged to be more recent and weaker ones to be older. In a previous example the different strengths of *beach* and *theorizing* may have enabled you to judge their relative recency.

According to the fourth, inference model, direct information about the time or age of events is seldom available; instead the time must usually be reconstructed through inference.[5] This model presupposes, quite reasonably, that we possess extensive knowledge of natural and social time patterns—patterns of seasons, holidays, meals, work schedules, presidential elections, and the like. It also assumes that we have memorized the dates of at least some important life events, such as graduations and birthdays. This general time knowledge must be distinguished from what we remember about the vast majority of specific experiences, which is likely to be a haphazard assemblage of information about place, activities, percepts, other people present, and so forth. Reconstruction is a matter of integrating these two sorts of information, much as archaeologists relate the findings of a dig to their knowledge of the ages of different pottery styles or metal technologies. If I can remember the weather, the location, or who was with me when a given event occurred, or that it was near the time of some other event whose time is known, I may be able to come up with a good estimate of when it must have been. Perhaps your impressions of how you recalled the time of your last visit to a museum fit this description; maybe you concluded that it must have been a Sunday, during a vacation, or when a particular friend visited.

A fifth way of representing temporal information in memory is to store the order of occurrence of many pairs of events.[6] Such order information could come about through a process described by the reminding model. This model assumes that new experiences call to mind previous, related events so that the order of the two is automatically stored. Such a process could bring about a large number of cross-referenced memories, and so an apt metaphor might be the references that appear in books like this one. A reader taking it out of the library could easily tell the order of publication of this book and those that are cited in it, even if the dates were somehow missing. This example also helps to illustrate an important point about the model: Just as I am very unlikely, as a psychologist, to cite works on medieval Spanish literature or DNA synthesis, so is order information unlikely to be available for unrelated events. One of the sample questions is particularly germane to this model. The ease with which you could probably order the Chernobyl and Three Mile Island accidents may be attributable to remembering Three Mile Island when Chernobyl was in the news and storing this fact. It might be more difficult to order Three Mile Island and the latest appearance of Halley's Comet (which are separated by about the same number of years).

It is relatively easy to think up possible models, but the real work comes from designing experiments to choose among them. In doing so, we discover the serious limits of the methods we have at our disposal—we have no direct measures of trace strengths, a biological time-tagging mechanism, or the organization of memory. We must conduct experiments and observations that only indirectly tell us what we want to know—in effect tricking the mind into giving up its secrets.

Testing the Models

The Time-Tagging Model

The first model we considered was the time-tagging model, in which the mind uses a kind of date-stamping machine to assign times to experiences as they occur. If the model strikes you as completely implausible, it is worth pointing out that there is some evidence that *place* is stored automatically for many or most experiences. Our ability to remember *where* a past event occurred is excellent,[7] and returning to the place where something was learned often helps people to recall it.[8] But as we will see, memory for exactly *when* something occurred is quite poor, and conversely giving someone a date seldom helps them remember what occurred at that time. Both of these points are nicely demonstrated in a study by the Dutch psychologist Willem Wagenaar.

Most psychological experiments are performed in a laboratory with a dozen or more subjects. But when we want to study memory over long periods, such as weeks, months, or years, laboratory methods become impractical, and we are left with two main alternatives: One is to ask subjects to recall news stories that would have reached large numbers of people about the time that they occurred. The other is for subjects to keep ongoing records of events in their lives and later have them attempt to remember the events. This latter approach was taken by Wagenaar, and given the huge investment of time required by such a study, it is not surprising that he used a small sample size— one (himself).

Beginning in 1978 and continuing over the following six years, Wagenaar[9] recorded the one or two "most remarkable" events that occurred each day, including information about what the event was, who was involved, where it took place, and its date. He tested his recall of this information when it was anywhere from less than half a year old up to five years old. In a predetermined order Wagenaar would read one randomly selected cue (*who, what, where,* or *when*) and then try to recall the other three. Next he gave himself a second clue, trying to remember the remaining items of information, and then a third clue, trying to remember the fourth.

Not surprisingly memories became less accurate with the passage of time, but there were interesting differences in how helpful the *who, what, when,* and *where* clues were, as well as in the difficulty of retrieving the four kinds of information. For example, *what* the event was proved to be the greatest help in retrieving other kinds of information, whereas *who* was involved and *where* it occurred were the easiest of the four to recall when the other clues were given. For our purposes the crucial findings were that providing the date was, as Wagenaar put it, "almost useless" in retrieving the other sorts of information and that memory for date was very poor when other cues were given. This second finding is quite consistent with the results of earlier studies: People can seldom recall the exact date of events from previous months or years. ("Exact" in Wagenaar's study was within one week of the true date. In most other studies it is defined as accurate to the month.)

If providing dates doesn't help access memories and providing descriptions doesn't lead to exact dating, it seems unlikely that the mind stores temporal information in the form of time-tags attached to individual traces. In fact the same conclusion can be drawn by a kind of exception that proves the rule. The neurologist Oliver Sacks[10] studied a pair of identical twins, both of them retarded and emotionally disturbed, who were able to perform remarkable feats of numerical insight, including recognizing novel eight-digit numbers as primes. Among their strange abilities was the capacity to recall what happened on particular days in their lives from about age four onward:

> Give them a date, and their eyes roll for a moment, and then they fixate, and in a flat, monotonous voice they tell you of the weather, the bare political events they would have heard of, and the events of their own lives—this last including the painful or poignant anguish of childhood, the contempt, the jeers, the mortifications they endured, but all delivered in an even and unvarying tone, without the least hint of any personal inflection or emotion. Here, clearly, one is dealing with memories that seem of a "documentary" kind, in which there is no personal reference, no personal relation, no living center whatever.

No one knows what processes underlie this uncanny ability to access memories by date, but it is so startlingly unlike normal time memory as to highlight the poverty of our date recall.

The difficulty that Wagenaar and most of us find in using and re-trieving dates should not lead us to conclude that memory is essentially devoid of time information. In fact the research literature is unanimous in showing that we can often remember the time of past events. But such memory tends to be approximate rather than precise.[11] This means that we need other models, ones that tolerate and perhaps even explain this imprecision.

The Temporal Sequence Model

Our second model can explain the approximate but imprecise nature of time memory and even can account for one of the patterns of inaccuracy. Recall that in the conveyor belt metaphor, time of occurrence is judged in terms of distance from the loading point, and position becomes more difficult to determine for distant parcels. This is just what we find in studies that have addressed the question: Dating errors increase as the true time that has elapsed increases.[12] Usually the magnitude of the error is in fact a fairly constant percentage of the age of the memory.[13]

There is an important exception to this rule, however, and it poses serious problems for the temporal sequence theory. In many studies of time memory, subjects are shown a list of words one at a time and then asked to estimate where individual words, sampled from the set, had occurred in the sequence. As the conveyor belt metaphor predicts, order judgments are most accurate for the last few words, with declining accuracy as one moves earlier in the list. However, a finding that cannot be explained by this model is that the *first* several words in the list are also quite accurately placed.[14] Instead of being difficult to discern, their position seems to stand out quite clearly. A related phenomenon is shown in experiments in which subjects are given several lists of words and then asked to remember in which list and where in the list a given word occurred. Subjects often assign words to the wrong list but get the "within list" position nearly right.[15] They seem to be remembering the nearness of these items to some temporal reference point, such as "beginning" or "end," rather than judging how far in the past the item occurred.

There are other laboratory findings that present problems for the temporal sequence theory, but one of Wagenaar's results is particularly convincing. On 157 days he recorded two events rather than the usual one. When each event came up during the recall part of the experiment, the test sheet told him that it was a "double," and he tried to recall the other event from the same day. Of the 314 recall trials he identified the corresponding event only 22 times. But 20 of these trials were from 10 days when both of the members were "clearly related by the location at which the events took place." Thus in only two cases were "unrelated" doubles recalled, leading Wagenaar to conclude that "contiguity in time is apparently not an effective cue for the retrieval of events." If Wagenaar's conclusion is correct, it seems very unlikely that memory is organized according to time of arrival.[16] This conclusion of course reduces the appeal of the temporal sequence model.

Strength Models

Strength theories, illustrated by our radioactive dating metaphor, have been particularly appealing to psychologists, I think, for two reasons: First, at an impressionistic level recent events usually seem more vivid than those of our distant past, particularly if the events we compare are of equal importance. This morning's breakfast is crystal clear compared with breakfast on a randomly chosen morning five years ago. If there are gradations to this vividness, we might have a rather nice way of judging the age of past events.

The second reason has more to do with issues that have been near the center of experimental psychology throughout its history. For more than a century, and from thousands of studies, we have known that the ability to recall experiences decreases in an orderly way with the passage of time. For example, in Wagenaar's study recall of information was about 70 percent correct for the most recent half year, but dropped to about 30 percent for memories that were five years old. One of the principal theories devised to explain this *forgetting curve* (figure 3.1) is that hypothetical entities called memory traces are laid down at the time of the initial experience, but, like radioactive sub-

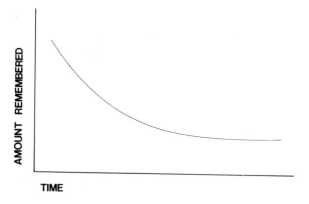

Figure 3.1
An idealized forgetting curve

stances, decay progressively with the passage of time. Thus Wagenaar's difficulty in recalling the older events would be attributed to the progressive decay of traces. Because this theory can explain the data from so many studies, it is tempting to extend it to account for time memory as well. We need only assume that people are capable of judging the strength of a given "trace" and using this information to localize the event in time.

In fact the strength model even has the advantage of explaining why dating accuracy is best for recent events, a phenomenon described when we considered the temporal sequence model. The sample forgetting curve shown in figure 3.1 illustrates that accuracy does not decline at a constant rate. Let's assume, as have most theorists, that trace strength shows the same pattern. For a while after the event occurs, trace strength declines quite rapidly. If we compare two events with ages that place them in this rapidly declining part of the curve, their strengths, and thus their ages, should be relatively easy to tell apart. But imagine another two events that have the same temporal separation as the first pair, but fall in the flatter part of the curve. They will differ little in strength, and we should therefore have greater difficulty deciding which is older. In this way the strength model can explain the increasing difficulty of dating older events, which has been shown repeatedly in studies of time memory.

With intuition, theoretical precedent, and a nice explanation on its side, what could be wrong with the strength model of time memory? One troublesome piece of evidence has already been presented. Recall that the first several words in a stimulus list can be localized in time better than those that fall in the middle of the list. This is hard to explain if trace strength is the cue, because older items are more likely to fall on the flatter, less discriminable part of the forgetting curve (see figure 3.1). There is a more serious problem, though, one that challenges the core assumption of the model. Part of the appeal of the strength model is its economy in using the same mechanism, decay of trace strength, to explain both memory loss with the passage of time and the ability to judge the time of past events. But the results of several studies challenge the assumption that a common mechanism could underlie memorability and time judgments.[17] In these experiments some words are deliberately made more difficult to recall than others. One way to accomplish this is by signaling to subjects immediately after each word appears whether they must remember the word. This leads subjects to rehearse some words but not others. Rehearsed words of course should have stronger traces, and indeed they are better recalled. But if strength is used to judge time of presentation, then more memorable words should also be judged to occur later in the list. However, this is not what we find. In fact the more memorable words are, the more accurately subjects judge their true time of presentation, whether it is the beginning, middle, or end of the list. Memorability and judged time do not seem to be based on the same information, and thus the apparent economy of the trace strength model is lost.

Before ruling out the strength model, three more points need to be raised in its defense: The first is that studies of time memory have not tested the model under optimum conditions, where one would expect real extremes of trace strength. Probably we could rapidly and very accurately decide which was older, a news headline that we heard during this morning's breakfast or one from five years ago. Second, I think nearly all psychologists would agree that we can distinguish information that is in short-term memory (the hypothetical memory system that allows us to remember telephone numbers long enough to write them down) from older information.

Third, if we modify the model slightly, there is evidence that information akin to strength *is* sometimes used to judge the time of past events. The modification and evidence come from the work of Norman Brown, Lance Rips, and Steven Shevell at the University of Chicago.[18] These researchers proposed that time is estimated not by assessing trace strength per se but by judging how much we know about an event. Because information is often lost with the passage of time (or at least becomes more difficult to get at), richness of information might provide an index of the age of a memory. This morning's breakfast might seem recent because we remember the coffee, the marmalade, and the wet newspaper. But breakfast five years ago seems very far in the past because we cannot recall anything about it.

To test their theory, Brown and his colleagues presented two groups of subjects with a set of 40 headlines, all from a nine-day period in 1982. The first group of subjects estimated how recently the events took place, whereas the second listed all the facts they could remember about the events. If the theory is correct, there should be a strong relation between how much group 2 recalled about particular events and how recent group 1 judged them to be: Better-recalled events should be judged to be more recent. This is exactly what was found. The judgments of which events were older by the first group were clearly related to the amount recalled about the events by the other group.

These findings support the theory that people use amount remembered as a clue to the age of an event. But the same study showed how unreliable this clue is. Even when the groups were tested immediately after the nine critical days, recency judgments were just barely more accurate than complete guessing (though as usual they appeared to be heavily influenced by the amount of information remembered about the events). The probable reason for the inaccuracy of this way of determining the time of events is that the passage of time is a less important influence on how much we recall about an event than how much we learned at the time that it occurred and how often we have thought of it since. Compelling events would be distorted toward the present if we relied very much on amount remembered.

People seem to sense the unreliability of amount remembered and to use other clues when they can. For example, in another experiment Brown, Rips, and Shevell[19] had subjects judge the dates of news events that were spread over a five-year period rather than a nine-day period. In this study subjects were very accurate in determining which events were older and which more recent. But they apparently did so with little help from amount remembered: There was a weak relation between how much they knew about the events and the dates assigned to them. This means of course that some other method must have been responsible for their success. Perhaps the knowledge assessment method is used only as a last resort, much as archaeologists rely on relatively inexact carbon dating methods only when they lack more dependable knowledge about the period associated with the artifacts of a given style.

The Inference Model

This use of inference to date artifacts is the metaphor used to illustrate our next model. According to the inference model, we use memory fragments to logically reconstruct when an event *must* have occurred.

Most of the evidence for the inference model is of a sort that makes psychologists uncomfortable. Around the turn of the century, the dominant way of studying mental processes was to have subjects, often the researchers themselves, report their thoughts as they solved some problem or considered some concept. This method, called *introspection*, produced a rich body of data, but much of the data seem to have been susceptible to distortion. For example, often the introspections of different theorists, although diverging from one another, showed all too tidy a fit to their own theories. For this reason there was a strong movement away from the introspective method. Even today most researchers report only their subjects' introspections alongside other more objective data, such as patterns of errors.[20]

Many of the studies of memory for the time of news events or personal events include descriptions of the methods that subjects claimed to use, in addition to the estimates themselves.[21] These reports are strikingly consistent with the inference model.

Table 3.1 gives examples of introspective reports from several of these studies. In many of the reports subjects seem to be estimating the date by trying to recall their own experiences at about the time that the events occurred. In other cases they appear to relate the event to another public event whose time is known (Camp David, the royal wedding). These are just the sorts of clues we would expect if people reconstruct the time of past events rather than simply mentally look up the date or try to judge the age of the memory. If the introspections could be taken at face value, the case for the inference model would be strong indeed.

Fortunately there is another kind of evidence for the model, one that is less vulnerable to charges of subjective distortion. The evidence involves what we will call *scale effects* in the accuracy of time

Table 3.1
Examples of Cues Reported in Remembering the Time of Past Events

---

Year and Month

It was a little while after Camp David, which was in '77, I'd say . . . February of '78. (Sadat and Begin win the Nobel Prize.)

It was within a few weeks of the birth of my first child.

Month

I was attending a once annual party.

It snowed in the morning.

The garden flowers were in bloom.

(Prince William [was] born) about a year after the July wedding.

They would have picked good weather for the launch. (The first astronaut sets foot on the moon.)

Day of the Week

It was definitely Friday because I remember collecting fish and chips for tea.

It was my wash day.

Time of Day

The Prince (Charles) stayed up all night. (Prince William is born.)

I knew it was in the afternoon because I skipped work between giving an anaesthetic to a sheep and preparing another for surgery.

Sources: Baddeley, Lewis, and Nimmo-Smith 1978, Brown, Shevell, and Rips 1986, Friedman and Wilkins 1985

memory.[22] Notice that in table 3.1 different sorts of cues were reported for judging year, month, day of the week, and time of day. Cues that would be helpful in remembering the year, such as the proximity to the birth of one's child, would be of little help in recalling the time of day, whereas many time-of-day cues, such as the place in one's daily work routine, would not help in inferring the year. If such clues are remembered in a haphazard way, as the inference model assumes, we would expect to find cases where people can judge the year very accurately, but have no idea about the time of day, or be accurate for hour, but off by months or years.

The latter finding would be especially interesting because it runs contrary to models that rely on trace strength or amount remembered: If our judgments were based on the age of a memory, how could we be accurate on a fine scale but inaccurate on a grosser scale? This would be like correctly estimating someone's height in the last fraction of an inch but being off by several inches.

A clear demonstration of scale effects in time memory comes from a study conducted at Oberlin College. On Friday, 31 January 1986 at approximately 11:50 AM, a mild but noticeable earthquake struck northeastern Ohio, where Oberlin is located. Most people experienced it as a vibration of the floor lasting a second or two. Earthquakes are quite rare in this part of the United States, so this was really quite a memorable, though harmless, event.

At the end of September 1986, I sent a survey to Oberlin College employees asking them to estimate the day of the month, day of the week, year, and hour that the earthquake occurred. They were asked to participate only if they had personally experienced the earthquake and to give their answers without first referring to a calendar or date book or consulting with anyone else.

The results showed remarkable accuracy for the time of day, even though the day of the week and day of the month were at about guessing levels, and month estimates were off by an average of nearly two months. The average hour estimate was off by just over one hour, a level of accuracy that would occur by pure guessing only one time in many thousands of repetitions of such an experiment. The fact that the earthquake occurred just before lunch time was fortuitous for testing the inference model, and more than half of the explanations offered for judging the hour involved some mention of the person's daily routine.

This study shows that inference plays an important role in our memory for the time of events, a role more significant than that played by trace strength or amount remembered. The inference model not only explains scale effects but can also account for several of the findings discussed previously. For example, the decline in the accuracy of temporal memory with the passage of time can be attributed to forgetting more and more of the fragments that would have been helpful in inferring the time. The unexpected accuracy shown for the first several words in a list can be explained simply by subjects associating those words with the beginning of the list itself, a kind of temporal landmark.[23] Thus the inference model has the hallmark of a good theory: It explains previous phenomena and predicts new ones.

The Reminding Model

The final model by no means contradicts the inference model, but it deserves discussion in its own right. In the reminding model many pairs of memories are cross-referenced like the citations in books, allowing us to determine which of the two memories is older. The most important prediction of the model is that pairs of thematically related events will be easier to order than unrelated pairs.[24] This prediction was tested in laboratory studies by Ovid Tzeng and Bill Cotton of the University of California, Riverside.

The basic procedure for one of Tzeng and Cotton's studies[25] is illustrated in table 3.2. Subjects were shown a randomly ordered sequence of 50 words for a few seconds each. The words were drawn from 10 different categories, similar to those used in our example. After viewing the sequence, subjects were given pairs of words and asked to judge which they had seen more recently. Half of the test pairs were made up of words from the same category, and half used words from different categories.

The reminding model predicts that same-category pairs will be easier to judge because it assumes, for example, that we are likely to remember *rose* when we get to *daisy* and to store this fact. This same sort of selectivity was presumably involved in our ease in ordering the Three Mile Island and Chernobyl accidents. Interestingly our first three models—the time-tagging, memory sequence, and strength models—could not explain this effect because they take a different stand on the source of temporal information in memory. In these three models the critical information is laid down when the event first occurs. But in the reminding model, temporal information about an item continues to be added to memory whenever it is "cited." Thus time memory is more like a scholar busily cross-referencing new sources to old than a clerk patiently recording each new acquisition.

Table 3.2
A Depiction of the Method Used for Testing the Reminding Model

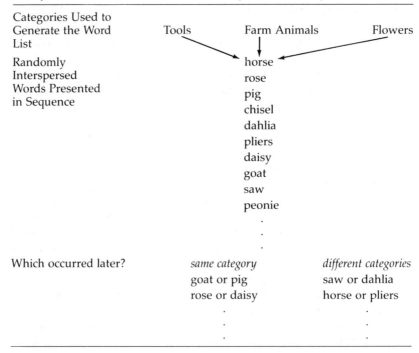

Categories Used to Generate the Word List	Tools	Farm Animals	Flowers
Randomly Interspersed Words Presented in Sequence		horse rose pig chisel dahlia pliers daisy goat saw peonie . . .	
Which occurred later?		*same category* goat or pig rose or daisy . . .	*different categories* saw or dahlia horse or pliers . . .

The results of the study supported the reminding model. Tzeng and Cotton's subjects scored better than chance (50 percent) in both situations, but were substantially better at ordering pairs of words from the same category (80 percent correct) than pairs from different categories (66 percent correct). This finding shows that old and new events do interact in memory, leading to the addition of information about their relative times of occurrence.

But how important is the reminding process in our memory for the time of past events? It is worth noting that even in experiments like Tzeng and Cotton's, judgments for different-category pairs are more accurate than pure guessing would allow.[26] This means that reminding cannot be the only process involved in time memory. For that matter it is not clear how this model would explain many of the results that we have already discussed, including the superiority of the earliest words on a list or scale effects in accuracy. Another limitation is that the reminding process seems better suited to judging the relative recency of two events than fixing single events in time. Relative recency might be of some use in judging dates, though, if we could relate the event in question to some other event whose time is known. The first example in table 3.1 illustrates just this sort of approach.

I suspect that the real importance of the reminding process is in helping us maintain temporal coherence in the thousands of separate strands that make up our lives.[27] I need to know something about the current condition of my car and what maintenance and repairs have been performed. I need to attend to the main life events of a substantial number of people—relatives, colleagues, former students, and so on. In international affairs, the arts, sports, science, and politics there are a great number of individual sequences that we keep track of. For all of these, order of the events is very significant, usually more important than exact dates. If we are able to remember old events when learning of new ones, and if these temporal direction markers can be stored, then we will have the raw materials needed to determine which state of affairs is current and what sequence has led up to it. In such a way a chaotic mass of recollections becomes thousands of individual stories (some more interesting than others, to be sure).

One Model or Many?

The human mind, like nature in general, stubbornly resists our metaphors. It would be satisfying at this point to embrace one of the models and conclude that time memory in fact resembles an archaeologist at work or the cross-references between books in a library. But it is probably wise, if unesthetic, to acknowledge that for the time being we will have to live with a mixed metaphor.

We saw that although there are serious deficiencies with our first two models (the time-tagging and temporal sequence models), the inference model, the reminding model, and the strength model all seem to explain how we *sometimes* get temporal information out of memory.[28] In fact it probably should have been obvious that more than one process is responsible for time memory. When I say that "It seems like just yesterday . . . ," I probably mean that the event appears recent because of its vividness (a kind of strength explanation), but that logic tells me that it must have been long ago (an inference explanation). For these reasons it is premature to gloss over the diversity of processes underlying time memory, and we will probably not understand time memory until we also understand when one or another process is most likely to be used.

The variation in processes is probably determined by the sorts of information that happen to be associated with the event in memory, an inherently fortuitous affair. Even exact dates are sometimes available (though other times embarrassingly unavailable) for weddings, graduations, birthdays, and other happenings where a certain amount of rehearsal has taken place. Other times order codes of the sort predicted by the reminding model will tell us all we need to know. As we have seen, this is especially likely if we are comparing the recency of two events that come from the same meaningful stream (like Chernobyl and Three Mile Island). The inference model of course emphasizes the haphazard quality of the cues that might be available, so when dates or order codes are absent, an almost unlimited variety of recollections might be sifted for their temporal value.

There are even occasions when nothing of temporal value can be found in memory itself, and we must resort to pure speculation, like luckless history students groping for the date of an unknown battle. Arnold Wilkins and I[29] sometimes found such an approach when we asked a group of British men and women to recall the time of a series of news events from the past decades. For some of the events on some of the scales, there was systematic distortion away from the true time and toward a more plausible time. For example, on 4 January 1967, in an event quite striking to many in Britain at the time, Donald Campbell was killed while attempting to set a water speed record on Lake Windemere. Our subjects, who estimated the time on several different scales, showed a strong tendency to distort their month judgments in the direction of summer, probably because few thought it likely that a water speed record would have been attempted in mid-winter. Perhaps it is most reasonable to think of speculation of this sort as merely an extreme case of inference, a point that should caution us about the veracity of answers to questions like Where were you on the night of . . . ?

Another likely influence on the processes used to recover temporal information is the amount of time we have available to make our judgment and the closely related matter of how important it is to be precise. I may be willing to rely on first impressions, perhaps based on trace strength, to pick a shirt I haven't worn for a while. But I will be far more circumspect, and probably engage in considerable reconstruction, before giving sworn testimony about the time of some event.

Obviously psychologists still face the challenge of sorting out when one or another process is most likely to be used and, by doing so, give a better answer to one of our original questions, How does time memory work? But the plurality of processes—the mixed metaphor—although esthetically displeasing, does have an important moral for another of our questions, Is time an automatic, fundamental property of memory?

The Place of Time in Memory

Nature might have provided us with a clear, dependable way of recording the time of events, an intrinsic temporal mnemonic code. Biological mechanisms control the timing of daily, monthly, and annual rhythms as well as growth programs lasting tens of years, so such a code would not be impossible. But we have found no evidence for its existence. Time memory seems more a makeshift affair, requiring a patchwork of processes and considerable effort—and usually ending in imprecision.[30] Each of the models that received support—the inference, strength, and reminding models—depends on indirect information about the time of events. In effect we are forced to construct a chronological past as best we can.

Certain other qualities appear to be far more fundamental in memory than time. In Wagenaar's study, for example, both location and the people involved could be recalled for large proportions of his life events, but exact time was very difficult to recover. Furthermore, as we saw previously, when two events of the same day could be linked, it was apparently nearly always on the basis of location. Emotion may be another distinctive and durable quality in memory.[31] Though there is some distortion with the passage of time, we seem to remember experiences as being frightening, joyful, embarrassing, and so forth over many decades.

All of this seems to lead to the conclusion that time is relatively insignificant information in the natural functioning of memory. Before accepting this conclusion, however, it is worth asking whether there might be a more natural temporal code that we have somehow overlooked. In some of the experiments that we have considered, subjects were led to think in terms of conventional units—calendar year, month, and sometimes date. In others they judged relative recency or position in a list. What nearly all of the studies have in common is a linear conception of time:[32] Time is an axis against which we plot accuracy, judged order of presentation, or trace strength; time is, in effect, distance from the present. But it is easy to overlook the fact that this conception of homogeneous, linear time is an intellectual construction, barely predating Newton's age, and could hardly have had any influence on the way the brain operates. Cyclic time appears a far deeper current in human experience and would have exerted a stronger force in shaping any natural temporal code.

Until quite recently the notion of universal, linear time was irrelevant to the lives of most of the world's peoples. Far more compelling than historical evolution or progress on a grand scale of time was the essential stability of things. Most important changes for our ancestors occurred on shorter time scales and were of a cyclic nature: the rising and setting of the sun; the seasons; and the cycles of birth, growth, and aging of successive generations. Adaptation depended on knowing the times for things within these cycles. The location of events in linear time was of little significance; such localization is confined to one experience and cannot be used more generally to guide future action.

To remember a location in cyclic time, one does not need an absolute time measure (of the sort that time-tagging or temporally sequenced memory could provide). Instead it is sufficient to store the fact that something occurred at about the same time as something else, as long as that "something else" can be located in a stable temporal pattern. Thus a hunter might remember that a particular animal approached a stream just before the sun set or someone who forages for roots and seeds might recall finding a ripe stalk of a certain grain around the time of the first frost. This kind of time memory of course can be explained by the inference model, and the examples here, except for content, resemble the introspective reports presented in table 3.1.

When linear time was needed, as in narratives, order of events would have been sufficient and absolute temporal localization unnecessary. The story of a hunt, for example, has its own internal time, which can be reconstructed from order codes, such as those assumed by the reminding model. Even when external temporal reference is needed, it is likely to be a matter of stepping from linear time to cyclic time ("When the sun rose on the next day . . . ," "When my son was an infant . . .") and back.

If this description is correct, then no intrinsic temporal code would have been needed to remember the location of events in cyclic time. The code would be the parts of cycles themselves—the rising sun, the coming frost—parts that impress themselves on us through repetition. Order codes in contrast may be a special adaptation, allowing us to keep track of the meaningful streams in our lives. But even they are by no means a natural code of uniform, linear time because the streams are largely isolated from one another.

It seems to be our nature to experience and remember time on different scales—in different cycles—or in isolated streams, not as an absolute, linear continuum. Relating memories to conventional linear time requires effortful processes like inference. When we allow our thoughts to follow their own course, however, they drift free from the constraints of linear time, washing from beaches of the present to beaches of the distant past.

Chapter 4

Representation

Mental Models of a Temporal World

If perception and memory were all we had to go on, our temporal world would be a strange one indeed. Not only would it be fraught with the distortions characteristic of time perception but there would be great holes left by the times when we sleep and perhaps even the times we are engrossed. Somehow, though, we manage to live in a much more uniform temporal world, one without holes or stretched or shrunken patches. Even more impressive is the fact that this idealized temporal environment can be manipulated in our minds at will. Far from being stuck in a world of immediate sensation, where changes unfold only at their own slow pace, we can instantly grasp patterns on the long scales of months and years and equally well move far into the future and the past.

We are able to manipulate time and make it uniform because we construct internal representations, or mental models, of time's structures. In this chapter I discuss what it means to say that we mentally represent time and what has been learned about these representations. Before looking at psychological approaches, however, several important points can be made by examining the devices that our culture uses to represent time.

Conventional Representations of Time

The clockface has become the dominant image of time, but if we look around us, we find other representations, numerous and varied. These range from the successive frames of comic strips to physicists' diagrams of relativistic space-time and include the circle of the zodiac, historical time lines, and train schedules along the way. Some are rich in their ability to capture time patterns, whereas others, like the digital display, are impoverished, but for all of them the purpose is to communicate temporal information. There are many kinds of temporal information, as we can see by examining several examples of conventional representations of time.

Figure 4.1
Detail of an early nineteenth century painting by J. A. Ersson, from Dalarna, Sweden (Courtesy of The Nordic Museum, Stockholm)

Figure 4.1 shows a Swedish provincial artist's depiction of the stages of men's and women's lives, in a form that has appeared in paintings since the seventeenth century and was common on calendars and other decorations in the nineteenth and early twentieth centuries. Though the symbolism of ascent and decline may no longer be popular, there is a distinctive way of capturing essentially continuous change through a succession of "snapshots," one for each decade. The main temporal information is the sequential order of a set of states from first to last. Sequential order is a frequent feature of many, but not all, conventional representations. For example, the verbal formula "Thirty days hath September, April, June, and November . . ." refers only to duration and says nothing about the order of the months. Duration of course is a separate form of temporal information.

Both nature and culture present us with another kind of time pattern—cyclic recurrence. Cyclic information is usually represented by circles, as on a clockface, but the waveforms of an oscilloscope or the succession of week rows on a calendar also capture it. Clocks and calendars also convey information about the hierarchical relations between different units: seconds, minutes, and hours for the former and days, weeks, and months for the latter. (Clocks do this awkwardly, I think, because the same space must be used for three scales.)

Scientific illustrations often depict time in a different way, as one axis on a two-dimensional plot. Figure 4.2, which shows changes in brain electrical activity after the presentation of a sound, is an exam-

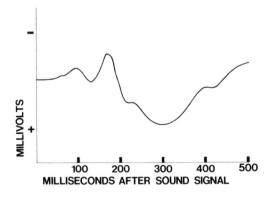

Figure 4.2
Idealized averaged evoked potential, showing changes in voltage recorded from scalp electrodes as a function of time after the presentation of the stimulus (Courtesy of Françoise Macar)

ple. These diagrams convey the information that time is a continuum, endlessly divisible, rather than a succession of states.

A final example illustrates still another kind of temporal information: Modern musical notation is rich in temporal information, including order, repetition, and relative duration—"relative" because different conductors may select different tempos, but a half note is always twice as long as a quarter note. But one additional kind of information that is made quite explicit is simultaneity. In figure 4.3 we see that the parts of different instruments are vertically aligned, so that a given place in the score means a single moment in time for all of the players. Anyone who has ever heard a beginners' band will know why simultaneity must be so precisely specified.

This commonsense look at conventional representations shows us that time can be thought of as information and that there are several distinct kinds of temporal information, including order, duration, recurrence, and simultaneity. We have also seen that different overt representations capture different sorts of information. Designing a representation seems to be a matter of trade-offs, with one kind of information emphasized at the expense of another. Calendars, for all their strengths, mask the continuous change from moment to moment that leads from one day to another. Musical notation emphasizes order, duration, and simultaneity, but repetition is only awkwardly portrayed. The idea that different forms of representation favor different kinds of information will be important when we turn our attention to mental representations.

Another observation we can hardly fail to make is the pervasiveness of spatial representations of time. There are exceptions of course, such as the verbal rule for the number of days in each month, our recitation of lists of the days of the week or months of the year, and literary metaphors for time. But the spatial arrangement of symbols is so frequent a format for representing temporal relations that one wonders whether there is something psychologically natural about it. The issue is related to the role of mental imagery in temporal thought, a topic treated in much of the remainder of this chapter. Even at an intuitive level, though, we can see why space is so successful a medium for modeling time. It allows us to freeze a succession of times that never, in reality, coexist. We can scan at will the parts in sequence, mimicking the passage of time, but are able to return again to the start or any other part of the pattern. With ease we can perceive relations that never could be experienced in the flow of time itself because only one part of a time pattern is ever available to sensation.

Figure 4.3
The opening measures of Mozart's *Gran Partita*, from a reproduction of the auto-graph manuscript (Courtesy of the Music Division, Library of Congress)

The Mental Representation of Time

External representations are tangible; we can see them or hear them and can describe their features in ways that leave little room for disagreement. But what do we mean when we refer to internal representations, and how could we ever reach a consensus about their nature? It is obvious that people carry around with them tremendous stores of knowledge—knowledge about places, social customs, language, the rules of baseball—but our methods for studying the nervous system are still far too limited to allow us to say anything useful about how this knowledge is represented. The mental representation of knowledge is encased in a black box, shielded from direct examination.

Black box mysteries are common in science, and many of our scientific heroes are admired for the progress they made in describing some phenomenon whose material basis lay beyond their reach. Gregor Mendel's landmark studies of inheritance of traits in peas, long before the discovery of the role and structure of chromosomes, is a familiar example. Important progress can be made far in advance of reductionistic description if one can come up with the right methods for shaking the black box, and—closely related—metaphors for thinking about its contents.

Cognitive psychologists shake the box by studying how subjects solve specially designed problems. The relative speed and accuracy with which different problems are solved and the answers themselves are used to infer what sorts of mental representations and processes could have led to this pattern of performance. The metaphors used to conceptualize the representation of knowledge (and to decide what sort of shaking to do) are varied: Mental representations are likened to pictures, to verbal propositions, to networks, to hierarchies, to lists, and so on. We needn't attempt a comprehensive description of methods and metaphors because our interest is in the representation of time patterns, and most of these metaphors have been fashioned to explore other contents. But the mental representation of time has received so little attention, has been such a fringe topic, that we have to borrow liberally from other areas of research.

Time and Mental Imagery

One metaphor for mental representation has appeared repeatedly in the past century in psychology and is in fact an ancient one in philosophy.[1] The idea is that mental images, akin in some senses to internal pictures, mediate some or all thinking. Most people have an intuitive appreciation of the notion of mental imagery. If you do not, try psychologists' favorite exercise for invoking the experience of imagery: Count from memory the number of windows in your house or apartment.

Imagery is usually associated with thinking about the appearance of familiar objects or spatial layouts, but it has sometimes been reported to play a central role in major discoveries in science and mathematics.[2] Einstein claimed that most of his important insights occurred in the form of images, including his famous thought experiment of traveling alongside a beam of light. Imagery does not seem to be restricted to the previously seen or even to the seeable, so we might well ask if it plays a part in the mental representation of something as abstract as time.

Reports of temporal imagery can be found in several publications of the late nineteenth century. Some were collected by Darwin's cousin Sir Francis Galton,[3] better known for his contributions to statistics and his pioneering (and crude) studies of the inheritance of intelligence. Galton reported that a substantial percentage of the people he surveyed claimed to use mental "number-forms," spatial representations of the relative positions of numerals, most arranged in one or two dimensions. A smaller number of similar images were reported for the alphabet, days, and months. In the 1920s J. P. Guilford, another researcher who later became famous for his work on intelligence, conducted a more systematic study of "spatial symbols in the apprehension of time."[4] He asked a group of undergraduates to describe and draw their representations of their own past, present, and future and of historical time. About 80 percent to 90 percent were able to provide drawings for each, though with varying degrees of difficulty. (Introspective studies always show considerable variation from one person to another in the vividness of imagery, and some people even deny possessing it.) The drawings were themselves heterogeneous, but a majority of the students used upward sloping forms to convey the progression of time. Guilford concluded that ". . . spatial images . . . carry the meaning of time and furnish a frame of reference for personal and historical time."

Other reports of temporal imagery[5] have appeared since these early studies, but the best introspective data come from recent studies by Philip Seymour and James Schroeder.[6] In both studies students were asked whether they had a visual image for each of several time scales and if so to draw it. The findings, summarized in table 4.1,[7] reveal that about three-quarters of the subjects claim to possess images of the time systems, and these images assume varied forms. Many of the images seem to show the influence of conventional representations—clockfaces for times of day, rows and columns for the year—

Table 4.1
Introspective Reports of Images of Time Expressed as Percentages

Content	Type of Drawing				Total Reporting Images
	Linear	Circular or Oval	Matrix	Other	
Time in a day	18	48	5	16	87
Days of the week	49	7	2	12	70
Months of the year	32	15	11	18	76
Seasons	18	29	10	25	82

Sources: Seymour 1980a, Schroeder 1980

but only about one-fifth of the subjects in Schroeder's study reported having been taught the image they used.

It is hard to know exactly what to conclude from these introspective studies other than that the experience of temporal imagery is common, probably occurring in a majority of people. In discussing memory, we saw that introspective evidence is not taken as decisive in itself, because we cannot be certain that subjects' reports really provide an accurate view of the processes they use in solving problems. In fact the studies I have described do not even involve solving problems, so we have no idea whether the images that subjects reported are simply associated with days, weeks, and years in some vague sense or whether they play an actual role in reasoning about time patterns.

Modern arguments for the existence of mental imagery, though, do not rest heavily on introspection nor, as we will see, need arguments for temporal imagery. Imagery researchers may be led to study the topic by their subjective experience of imagery and even rely on this experience in designing their studies, but their public evidence takes the form of patterns of response times on laboratory tasks. To understand their methods, it is necessary to say a little more about the imagery metaphor.[8]

The first thing that must be said about the imagery metaphor is that its advocates realize it is just a metaphor—no one believes that there are literally pictures inside our heads. Furthermore, although we have reason to believe that certain brain structures play a special role in imaginal thinking, the metaphor itself is not cast in neurological terms. In fact it is really quite the most self-conscious of metaphors; exponents repeatedly use such phrases as *as if* or *analogous to* or *in the same way that*. The metaphor is that we represent certain information in a form resembling pictures and operate on these representations by means of processes resembling visual perception. Contemporary imagery theorists believe that mental images are only one of several forms of representation, usually contrasting it with a form closer to language.

The evidence for imagery gains its meaning from the underlying analogy: Problem solving by means of imagery is shown to resemble the perception of pictures. Of the many clever experiments using this so-called analog approach, my favorite is a study by Allan Paivio[9] of the University of Western Ontario, which, coincidentally for us, uses clocks as stimuli. Paivio asked his subjects to imagine a pair of clock-faces and to judge which clock's hour and minute hands would form a smaller angle. The times for the two clocks were given digitally. You may want to try the following three examples: (a) 3:40 versus 9:55, (b) 2:35 versus 8:00, and (c) 4:50 versus 1:10. For each of these pairs the smaller acute angle would be made by the second clock's time. These examples should give a feel not only for the task but also for the fact that problems vary in their difficulty. Most people would find problem c to be easier than problem b. These two problems differ in the magnitude of the *difference* between their angles: 25 minutes (150°) for problem c and 5 minutes (30°) for problem b. (Problem a falls in between, with a difference of 15 minutes [90°].) It is this effect of the difference between the angles that provides the crucial link between the comparison of mental clocks and the perception of pictures. If the pairs of angles to be compared were presented as pictures instead of as digital times, we would expect the fastest responses and greatest accuracy to occur when the differences between the angles were large. Showing the same effect for imagined clocks would demonstrate an important similarity between mental operations and perception and thus bolster the imagery metaphor.

In Paivio's study the subjects were shown 40 pairs of digital clock times. For each pair they pressed a key underneath the time they judged to make a smaller angle. The pairs were selected to have differences between the two angles of 30°, 60°, 90°, 120°, and 150°. The average times taken to respond to problems of each amount of difference between the angles are shown in figure 4.4. We see that problems become easier (as reflected by more rapid responses) when pairs differ more in their angles. These results demonstrate that some mental comparison is affected by difference between the angles in the same way that we would expect a visual comparison to be affected. This leads to the conclusion that image representations are involved in solving this task. Incidentally the subjects in this experiment overwhelmingly reported using images to solve the problems.

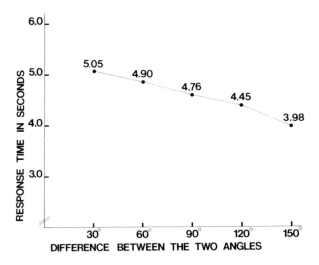

Figure 4.4
The average amount of time taken to compare clock hands of different angles in Paivio's experiment

Studies like Paivio's demonstrate the value of the imagery metaphor: It predicts a number of interesting phenomena that do not follow from the other main metaphors in cognitive psychology. But the case for temporal imagery cannot rest on demonstrations of imagery for contents that are not themselves temporal patterns. Paivio's choice of clocks for his stimuli had nothing to do with temporal representation; clock times simply provided an elegant way of precisely specifying spatial configurations. His study, like the majority of studies using the analog approach, bears on the role of imagery in reasoning about spatial relationships. Thus we turn next to several studies in which I have applied the analog approach to reasoning about the days of the week and months of the year.[10]

The first experiment has a rationale similar to that of Paivio's study, but here the subjects compared intervals of months instead of angles made by clock hands. For example, in one problem they were asked to decide which temporal interval is shorter, December to June or August to November. (The problems assumed continuity between one year and the next, so the correct answer is the second pair.) Here are a few additional examples if you wish to see what it is like to be a subject in this experiment: (a) December to May versus July to October, (b) November to April versus May to September, and (c) October to April versus November to January. The correct answer to each problem is again the second pair.

Notice that these problems, like Paivio's, seem to vary in difficulty. Problem b is likely to have been relatively difficult and problem c relatively easy. Of these three problems, c has the greatest *difference* in interval lengths (four months), b the least difference (one month), and a fell in between (two months). If the imagery metaphor applies to this task, problems in which the pairs differ most in interval length should be easiest to solve. By analogy, if we were making a visual comparison of the lengths of two lines, our task would be easiest when one line was much longer than the other.

To test this prediction, I asked a group of students to solve 80 problems of the sort that we have just seen. The interval pairs were selected to differ by 1, 2, 3, or 4 months, and the four types of problems were randomly interspersed. Figure 4.5 shows the average response times for each of the four interval differences. As the image metaphor predicts, problems with the smallest interval difference were the most difficult. The shape of the curve in figure 4.5 indicates that problems did not get any easier beyond interval differences of 3 months; when the intervals differed by this much, subjects were able to solve the problems very rapidly. A comparison of the number of errors for the four problem types showed the same pattern: Errors were most common for differences of 1, decreased to differences of 3, and then leveled off. This kind of leveling-off pattern is common in perceptual discrimination tasks, where beyond a certain point the comparison itself becomes negligibly easier.

When the experiment was over, subjects were asked to report the methods they had used in solving the problems. The most common

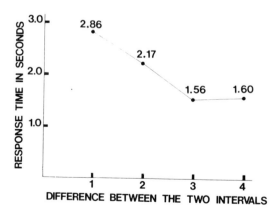

Figure 4.5
The average amount of time taken to compare pairs of month intervals as a function of the difference between the interval lengths

responses involved imagery. For example, one subject said, "I thought of them laid out on a rule with one month taking up one inch. Then I would think of the intervals and which would have a shorter line segment . . ." As in Paivio's study the introspections converge with pattern of response times and errors in supporting the imagery metaphor.

This experiment shows not only that time patterns can be represented as images but also that these images play a functional role in thinking about the months of the year. The magnitude of the intervals separating different months is information, and images provide a way to extract that information. A similar study with similar results showed that imagery captures information about the days of the week as well. No doubt mental imagery serves us in our day-to-day thinking about numerous time patterns, freeing us from our bondage to the present and allowing us to "see" relations between widely separated times.

Before we leave the topic, I want to describe one other demonstration of temporal imagery, using a method called *direction judgments*. This experiment illustrates that very different kinds of operations can be performed on representations of the months and shows quite directly the similarity between temporal and spatial representation. To understand the logic of the experiment, consider first the following hypothetical task (which has never been used in an experiment, so far as I know): Figure 4.6 depicts twelve lightbulbs arranged in a circle. On a given trial two of the bulbs are illuminated in sequence. The task is to decide as rapidly as possible whether the second bulb is closer to the first by moving in a clockwise or counterclockwise direction from the first. For example, if the sequence were k–c, the correct answer would be clockwise. If the sequence were f–a, it would be counterclockwise. Figure 4.6 gives some sample problems, which are certainly easy, but see if you can get some idea of what sorts of problems are relatively more difficult than others. I think that under conditions where time was at a premium, responses would be somewhat slower on problems where the two bulbs were separated by nearly 180°. If this assumption is correct, it suggests another analog task that is particularly well suited to demonstrating images of cyclic patterns.

The task is to present two elements of a cycle and ask subjects to decide in which direction the second element is closer to the first. In the direction judgment experiment that I describe here, subjects received two month names in sequence and had to decide whether the second month was closer to the first by going *forward* or *backward* in time. For example, for the pair November–February the correct an-

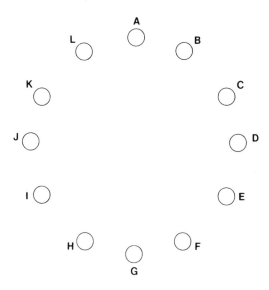

SAMPLE PROBLEMS

1. G–I
2. E–J
3. B–E
4. D–K
5. C–D
6. C–H

Figure 4.6
A circular arrangement of light bulbs and some sample problems in a hypothetical
perception experiment

swer would be forward. For the pair October-June the correct answer
would be backward. Here are a few more problems, if you wish to
try them: (a) December-July, (b) February-June, (c) May-August, (d)
September-February, and (e) April-December. (The correct answers
are (a) backward, (b) forward, (c) forward, (d) forward, and (e) backward.) The most difficult problems, if the analogy with the perceptual
task is valid, should be the ones where the separation between the
months is close to 6 months, such as problems a and d in these
examples.

There was another part to the experiment, one that applied the
direction judgment method to the representation of spatial knowledge. This task was included because many researchers have argued
that spatial relations are often conceptualized through mental im-

agery. Paivio's clock task showed one example of spatial imagery; another would be thinking about the route from your house to the grocery store. The direction judgment method requires a roughly circular arrangement of locations, so I chose as content twelve buildings that are about equally spaced, three to a side, around a large campus square in Oberlin. Students who were familiar with the locations of all of the buildings received pairs of building names and judged whether the second building was closer to the first by going clockwise or counterclockwise around the perimeter of the square. Again the analogy to our hypothetical perception experiment suggests that pairs close to the 180° "boundary" will be the most difficult to judge. If both spatial and temporal judgments are influenced by the same factor—proximity to the 180° boundary—we will have even greater reason to believe in the reality of temporal imagery.

In the temporal part of the experiment, 120 pairs of month names were flashed on a computer screen, and for each pair subjects pressed one of two buttons, depending on whether the second month was closer to the first by going forward or backward in time. In the spatial part 120 pairs of building names appeared, and the buttons corresponded to clockwise and counterclockwise directions. The results are depicted in figure 4.7. The vertical axis shows response times, and the horizontal axis shows how close the second month or building is to the "boundary" (180° from the first month or building). The analog prediction is clearly upheld for both contents: The slowest responses occurred near the boundary. The number of errors revealed the same

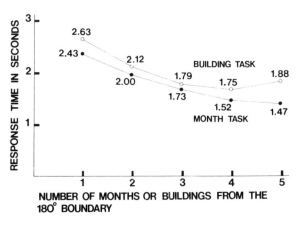

Figure 4.7
The average amount of time taken to decide in which direction a month or building is closer as a function of distance from the 180° boundary

pattern, as did the response times and errors in a second experiment using days of the week as stimuli.

Taken together with the studies in which subjects compared two intervals, these results show that imagery is an important way of representing temporal information. The value of imagery for conceptualizing temporal relations is probably the same as its value for thinking about space: The flexibility with which different relationships can be detected. These relationships might well have been represented in memory as individual facts (or *propositions*, as psychologists call them), such as "the interval from May to August is three months" or "March is closer to December in the forward direction," which we simply look up mentally when the appropriate situation arises. However, this would require a very large number of propositions for each content—months, days of the week, buildings around the campus square and so forth—and the vast majority of these propositions would never be used. One could go through a whole lifetime without comparing two intervals of months, and even lifelong residents of Oberlin have probably never wondered whether one building is closer to another in the clockwise or counterclockwise direction (to find the shortest route, they would simply cut across the square!). Imagery, like its metaphorical relative, visual perception, allows one to "see" relations that have never been noticed before. Rather than storing information about each possible relation, it seems that we are able to construct images that are tailor-made to the demands of particular problems.

Verbal Coding of Temporal Order
The imagery metaphor is only one of many that have been proposed to describe mental representation, and there is no reason why temporal information should be represented in any single way. If different forms of internal representation, like our external ones, have their strengths and weaknesses, then having multiple ways of representing time should be a clear advantage. Several of the alternatives to imagery are metaphors based on language rather than on perception. In these metaphors information is stored in forms resembling words or sentences.

One language-based metaphor, which I call the verbal list metaphor, seems particularly promising for storing information about temporal order. When we must memorize the order of some set of elements, we often resort to mnemonics using a sentence or song. For example, medical students learn rhymes, often bawdy, to memorize the order of the cranial nerves,[11] and we are all familiar with the

"ABCs song" used by children to memorize the order of the letters of the alphabet. The verbal list metaphor is simply that the representations underlying these mnemonics are like chains of names, each linked to the next from start to finish.[12] It is assumed that when such representations are used, the elements are actually activated one after the other, just as the words would be said one after another if the list were recited aloud.

This sequential activation of elements is what makes these representations particularly useful for getting at temporal information, and it is also one of the main characteristics that researchers look for when they are trying to determine whether this kind of representation is being used. Sequential activation is useful because it allows us to determine "distances" rather precisely. If I want to know what month is three months after May, it would be nice to have discrete mental events (activating the months after May) that I can count. We saw that exact distances were difficult to determine through imagery, but here is a representation that could be used when precision is needed.

Sequential activation is easily detected in laboratory tasks. If we give subjects problems in which they must judge various distances between elements, response time will increase continuously as the distance to be judged increases. Note that this property would not be expected from all types of representations. For example, multiplication problems do not show large differences in solution times as we go from 3 × 3 to 4 × 4 to 5 × 5, because we do not have to activate each intervening number to reach the answer.[13] But there is a strong effect of "distance" when subjects are asked to give the letter that comes a certain number of steps after another in the alphabet (for example, What comes six letters after F?). In one of my experiments it took subjects nearly two seconds longer to judge six-letter than three-letter separations.[14]

The same sorts of effects have been found for judgments of the separation of months of the year and days of the week.[15] Here are some sample problems of different distances: Name the month that is two months after (a) June, (b) October, (c) March. Give the month four months after (d) February, (e) August, (f) April. (The answer to problem a is August and to problem d is June.) In several experiments using these sorts of problems, subjects needed an additional half second or so for each additional month or day in the interval. If you were like a typical subject, problems d through f would have taken about a second longer to solve than problems a through c.

The clear distance effects found for day of the week and month problems are one line of evidence for the verbal list representation of temporal information. Two others came from the same studies: First, in some of these experiments subjects were asked to explain how they solved the problems.[16] The majority reported saying the intervening months to themselves, which is just what we would expect from the verbal list metaphor. Very few claimed to use imagery on these problems. Another kind of evidence is that subjects were much faster in judging forward intervals (as in our examples) than backward intervals[17] (for example, what month is four months before July?). This kind of asymmetry is expected because direction is such an important characteristic of language. (Try reciting your favorite poem backward!)

The Meaning of Time

Having established the value of the imagery and verbal list metaphors, we might reasonably ask whether these two are sufficient to describe our knowledge of time. I think that the answer is no. A little reflection shows that we know a good deal more about time than the order of the elements of conventional time systems. The months and days themselves are hardly the abstract time markers my discussion has made them out to be. Rather they are infused with meaning—of drudgery or celebration, or regimentation or freedom, of biting cold or mildness and fragrance. Many of these meanings are intensely personal, as we see from the depression that some people feel each year around the anniversary of the loss of someone they loved. But several studies have shown that associations are often shared as well.

Philip Seymour, whose work was discussed, asked a group of 100 Scottish students to report colors and other associations to the months and seasons.[18] Not surprisingly green, yellow, and blue were frequently given for the spring and summer months, brown for autumn, and white and gray for the winter months. Associations to seasons included climate and vegetation as well as activities, holidays, and moods.

Feelings about the months have also been studied using a method called the *semantic differential*.[19] In this method subjects rate concepts by making a mark somewhere on a line whose ends are labeled by opposite qualities (for example, pleasant versus unpleasant or relaxed versus tense). When the months are rated by students, a clear pattern emerges: Pleasantness increases gradually from January through the spring months, peaks from May through July, drops through the autumn months, and finally rebounds in December. The pattern of course reflects students' attraction to the vacation months, with other months gaining value by their proximity and losing it by their distance. December holidays and vacation bring another focal point to the year, though one whose influence does not spread to adjacent months.

These few examples—feelings, activities, holidays, climate—show the wealth of information we possess about temporal elements. But it is a different kind of information than was captured by the image and verbal list metaphors. Image and verbal list representations simulate the structure of time and appear to stand apart as models of a year, a week, or a day. In contrast time elements have meaning because they are richly connected to our general store of knowledge.

The rich interconnections of ideas in human memory—so evident in the drift of ideas that we experience in the stream of consciousness experience—is often described by psychologists by the metaphor of a *semantic network.*[20] According to this metaphor, meaning is made up of units or parcels that resemble concepts or sentences. These parcels are interconnected through a vast network of links such that any two parcels are more or less closely connected with one another. It is easy to imagine how time elements could be embedded in such a network. July, for example, might be closely linked to parcels representing *hot, Independence Day, pleasantness,* and *June,* more distantly linked to *Julius Caesar,* the birthday of a slight acquaintance, and so forth.

So far there has been little direct evidence to support such a representation of temporal knowledge, but the theory has been so productive in describing other areas of knowledge that it seems likely to apply to time as well.[21] Furthermore there appears to be no need for special kinds of mental representations to capture temporal meanings, as there had been for representations of temporal structure. The association between *July* and *hot* seems much the same sort of information as the link between *desert* and *hot.*

The Portability of Time

Having shaken the black box in various ways, we find that no single metaphor suffices for describing its contents. In some ways the situation resembles physicists' understanding of the nature of light: Paradoxically, depending on how the black box is shaken, wave or particle metaphors provide a better account. But in the case of temporal representation, multiplicity is probably more a lesson than a paradox. To understand our temporal environment, we must capture the information in many different kinds of patterns, and even what seems to be a single pattern (for example, the months of the year) is really composed of several different kinds of information (the order of the elements, their separations, and their meanings). Although few have been studied, I suspect that we possess a large repertoire of mental representations of time patterns, and that it is these collectively that account for our power in manipulating and understanding time.

Whatever particular information they capture, all of these representations are abstractions—idealized models—that free us from the imperfections of time perception and memory and the constraint of living at a single point in a gradually changing world. The representations are carried around with us like the watches we use to simulate the rotation of the earth. But insofar as they are abstract models of time, they have one limitation that no useful clock does—they do not tell us what time it is now. Like maps these representations tell us nothing about our present location. This is a problem we turn to next as we consider the nature of temporal orientation.

Chapter 5

Orientation

Constructing a Place in Time

From personal experience I may say that regression to temporal norms less elaborate than our own is an entirely painless and not unpleasant process. During the summer of 1932, when I spent most of my time up the Berens River [in Canada] with the Pekangikum Indians, I lost track of the days of the month, since I did not have a calendar with me; the days of the week became meaningless, since, in two settlements, there were no missionaries and hence no Sunday observance or other activities that differentiated one day from another and, as my watch stopped running, I had no way of keeping track of the hours of the day. My "disorientation," of course, was only such relative to the reference points of western civilization to which I was habituated. Once the usual mechanical and institutional aids to these were removed, the relativity and provinciality of western time concepts became obvious.

This excerpt, from a study by the anthropologist Irving Hallowell,[1] describes a kind of prolonged disorientation from conventional time that few of us ever experience. Normally our cultural time system is like an aura that surrounds us, a seldom-noticed but nonetheless compelling framework within which our lives unfold. We have a sense of place in time that rivals our sense of place in space. Yet Hallowell's report shows just how ephemeral temporal orientation can be. Remove the usual supports, and the surrounding framework collapses.

In this chapter we consider the psychological processes that lead to this habitual but mysterious ability to know our place in time. Not surprisingly the ability is related to time perception, memory, and representation, which we discussed in the preceding chapters. But there is also something special about temporal orientation: It combines the dynamism of an ever-changing present (which of course is central to perception and memory) with the unchanging relations between time markers (which is a characteristic of representations).

Temporal orientation may reasonably be defined as the ability to determine the current time and the relative times of other events with respect to some temporal framework.[2] To be temporally oriented, we need to be able to identify the present time (for example, to know that today is Thursday), but we also need to know where that time falls relative to other time markers and important events (that our present day is after Wednesday, near the end of the work week, and so forth). By analogy spatial orientation involves more than the ability to give one's present address; it is important to know where we are relative to other places.

Another central property of temporal orientation that is shared with our sense of position in space is that we can be oriented (or disoriented) on many different scales. We can know our position within our room, building, neighborhood, city, or country, but are almost never oriented on all of these scales at once. Similarly, temporal orientation must take place separately on the scales of time of day, day of the week, month or season of the year, and perhaps even parts of a lifetime.

Temporal orientation is normally a rapid and unnoticed process. If you stopped someone on the street to ask, "What day is today?" you would have your answer in about one to two seconds. What happens during that interval of course is what we need to explain if we are to understand the ability to know one's place in time. Do we rely mainly on cues in the environment, or do we instead consult internal sources of information? If we do depend on internal information, how are we able to update it so that we do not, for example, give some previous day as the answer?

What Sources of Information Are Available?

To answer these questions, it is useful to first consider what sorts of information *might* be used to know our place in time. As we have already seen, two main categories of information are required for temporal orientation—dynamic and stable information. Dynamic information is needed to tell the current time from other possible times, and stable information is needed to know where different times *always* fall relative to one another.

Dynamic information might come in any of several forms: First, we might be able to reckon the present time by judging how long it has been since some "landmark" (say, breakfast or Sunday). Second, we could try to use our current environment or activities (for example, how bright it is outside or whether we are at work or at home) as clues to what time it *must* be. A third possibility is that we simply remember the most recent time cue (the noon bells, the fact that my appointment calendar read Thursday the last time I looked) and assume that this time is still more or less correct.

But each of these seemingly straightforward approaches actually requires more elementary processes, raising even more questions about how temporal orientation could work. Judging the amount of time that has elapsed since some landmark could involve many of the numerous processes we considered in our discussions of duration perception and time memory (for example, considering the amount of detail remembered about breakfast or the number of mental and external events that seem to have transpired since then). To infer the time from present clues, we need ways to select useful evidence from the multitude of possible information, compare it with our knowledge of the characteristics of particular times, and decide which time is the best match. Even remembering the most recent time cue requires some way of distinguishing what we learned a relatively short while ago from what we learned in previous hours or days.

As we saw in chapter 4, stable information can also come in many forms, including images, verbal lists, and associative networks. This variety raises many possibilities about how we are able to understand our location in time relative to other times. Do we think of our proximity to the weekend by constructing an image of our position within the week, counting off the days until Saturday, or in some other way? For that matter we can ask what role stable information plays in determining the present time. Networks of associations may be used to match current activities and events to the label *Thursday,* or we may even use images as a first step to get a rough feel for where we are within the week. Clearly we need some way of choosing among these many alternatives. Two kinds of evidence are particularly useful for this purpose—studies of normal temporal orientation and the examination of cases of disorientation.

What Day Is Today? Experiments on Temporal Orientation

As important as temporal orientation is in our daily lives, it is one of the least studied topics in the psychology of time. Virtually all that we know about normal orientation comes from just three experiments,[3] conducted by Asher Koriat and his colleagues and Benny Shanon, and all pertain exclusively to orientation within the week. If we must have information about only one time scale, though, the week is a fortunate choice. This is because the seven-day cycle is entirely a matter of social convention, and there are few immediate cues to the present day. You can look out the window and see that it is daytime or winter, but it would be harder to tell that it is Monday or Thursday. Orientation within the week must therefore be rather different from spatial orientation, where looking around helps us to know where we are. Instead it may be more like trying to know our place by considering where we were and where we are going.

In the three studies large numbers of passersby were asked, in one way or another, to judge their current location within the days of the week, while the experimenters recorded the time taken to respond. (Passersby were used because subjects who sign up for laboratory experiments tend to select convenient, and therefore possibly unrepresentative days.) The basic method was to ask "What day is today?" on different days of the week or at different times of day. But there were also two variations on this procedure. One was to include questions about yesterday and tomorrow. The other was to ask subjects to judge as true or false statements like *Today is Monday* (or Tuesday and so forth) on different days of the week. This seemingly peculiar task allows one to address questions such as whether, in deciding what today really is, it is easier to rule out some days than others.

Given the large amount of effort that went into these studies, it is particularly gratifying that they produced some rather informative results. The main findings include

1. It is easier to identify "today" during or near the weekend than in the middle of the week.
2. Reports of identifying "today" by thinking about "yesterday" decline from Monday to Friday, whereas those involving thinking about "tomorrow" increase.
3. In the morning it is easier to identify "yesterday" than "tomorrow." In the evening "tomorrow" is easier to identify than "yesterday."
4. Around noon on Monday and Tuesday, it is easier to identify "yesterday" than "tomorrow." Around noon on Wednesday, Thursday, and Friday, it is easier to identify "tomorrow" than "yesterday."
5. It is easier to rule out incorrect days when they fall during or adjacent to the weekend than when they fall in the middle of the week.
6. Incorrect near days are usually more difficult to rule out than incorrect far days. Similarly errors in identifying "today" more often are near days than far days.

I examine each of these main findings in turn and consider what they tell us about the process of temporal orientation. Most of the phenomena concern the relative difficulty of different questions asked at different times. (For our purposes *easier* means that subjects responded more rapidly, made fewer errors, or both.)

Weekends as Landmarks
The first point concerns the relative difficulty of identifying "today" on different days of the week. Imagine that you were asked, "What day is today?" on several different days of the week. On which days do you think it would be especially easy to tell? The clear result of all three studies was that people find it easier to name "today" when they are tested near the weekend than when they are asked on a midweek day (figure 5.1). Actually the exact pattern differed somewhat between the studies, because two of them were conducted with Israeli students (for whom Saturday is the only full day of rest and Sunday is an ordinary work day) and the other study (the one from which the data in the figure are drawn) with American students (who have a two-day weekend of Saturday and Sunday). Friday was an easy day to identify in both cultures, but Monday was about as difficult as other midweek days for the Israeli samples.

The simplest way to describe these findings is to say that temporal

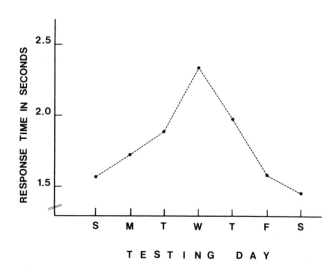

Figure 5.1
The time taken by American students to answer the question *What day is today?* on different days of the week (Source: Shanon 1979)

orientation is facilitated by proximity to the weekend. But why should this be? One reason could be that we are somehow mentally fresher around weekends and thus answer all sorts of questions more rapidly. This possibility can be ruled out, however, because the studies found no day-to-day differences in answering nontemporal control questions such as *Name a country beginning with the letter G.*

Another, more interesting response is that weekends serve as landmarks for orienting within the week.[4] For something to be a literal landmark, it must be easy to recognize and its position in space must be well known. This metaphor of spatial landmarks would seem to suit weekends well, in that they are highly distinctive (for example, they are filled with sports events, socializing, and other activities that do not occur on other days) and their position within the week is well known (as the term *weekend* implies). Thus, if it is currently Saturday, all we need to do is recognize some distinguishing feature of Saturdays, and we will be oriented. But how, in the case of days just after or just before the weekend, can something that has already occurred or has not yet occurred influence our ability to orient in the present? These cases are more like orienting in space before we can yet see the landmark or after we have left it behind us.

For a landmark hypothesis to explain the ease of orientation on these days, we would need to assume more than just the distinctiveness of weekends and their clear locations in time. We would also need some way of using currently available information to relate the *present* to the weekend landmark. In spatial orientation a sign saying that Paris is 20 kilometers in a particular direction is nearly as helpful as being in Paris itself. What sorts of cues in the present could point toward other times with equal clarity?

Some pointers to the weekend could be provided by our environment, such as the unusual rush of drivers on Fridays leaving the city for the weekend or the summary of football scores we hear on the Monday morning news. Others, however, may reside in the current and recent contents of consciousness. On Monday we may have particularly vivid recollections of the weekend, perhaps aided by rehearsal of its most salient events. On Friday the nearness of the weekend may lead to frequent thoughts of what the weekend holds in store for us. The frequency and recency of these thoughts would make them especially easy to access when one begins searching in memory for information that could help decide between different days of the week. Of course we must have some way of distinguishing memory from anticipation, or else we would be prone to confuse, say, Friday with Sunday.

Several of the other results of the temporal orientation experiments provide support for the idea that the changing contents of consciousness help us to orient by providing pointers to other times. Point 2 in the list refers to subjects' explanations of how they arrived at their answer to the question, What day is today? Just after the weekend there is a tendency to think of the previous day in deciding what "today" is, whereas just before the weekend "tomorrow" is a more likely clue. Presumably the events of Sunday and their recent pastness are especially clear on Monday. Similarly on Friday it is easy to remember having thought about the close futurity of Saturday.

Interestingly this same sort of fluctuation in the forward-looking and backward-looking quality of consciousness is seen not only in transitions to and from the weekend but in the more mundane transitions from one day to the next. Point number 3 describes the responses to the questions, What day of the week was yesterday? and What day of the week will tomorrow be? (The two questions were asked of different groups of subjects.) We see that "yesterday" is especially easy to identify in the morning (7:00 to 9:00 AM in this experiment), and "tomorrow" is especially easy to name in the evening (9:00 to 11:00 PM). These results probably reflect the fact that thoughts of the identity and pastness of "yesterday" decline from morning to evening, while thoughts about "tomorrow" increase.

If we take a sort of neutral point in the day, we can see another phenomenon similar to that described in point 2. Point number 4 in the list refers to the relative difficulty of "yesterday" and "tomorrow" questions when asked between noon and 2:00 PM on different days of the week. For the American subjects who served in this experiment, "yesterday" was especially easy to identify during the first two weekdays, and "tomorrow" was especially easy during the last three weekdays. Apparently as the week goes on there is something of a shift from backward-looking thoughts to forward-looking thoughts.

Points 2 and 4 help us to understand how the weekend could be a landmark for temporal orientation on other days of the week. Because we live in the present of course there is no physical evidence of our position relative to another time. But the social construct of weekends is such a powerful influence on our activities and motivation that weekend-referring thoughts occur throughout the week. These thoughts change from day to day, providing a rather direct sense of the distance and direction of weekend days, particularly on days adjacent to the weekend.

This landmark hypothesis is intuitively appealing and seems consistent with points 1, 2, and 4 in the list. However, the hypothesis, as we have formulated it, leaves an important question unanswered: Why is there a decrease in backward-looking thoughts and an increase in forward-looking thoughts as the week goes on? Without specifying the source of change, there is a troubling circularity to the hypothesis: We use our weekend-referring thoughts to determine the current day, but some sense of where we are in the week is needed for us to have the appropriate thoughts.

The decrease in backward-looking thoughts as the week goes on might be explained simply by the fading of weekend memories with the passage of time. (This explanation incorporates the first of our possible sources of dynamic information.) By the time Wednesday rolls around, the weekend is a dim memory, and relatively bland Monday and Tuesday provide few reasons to think about the past. However, the workings of memory can hardly account for the progressive increase in the pull of future events. To know on Friday that it is time to start anticipating our weekend activities, we would need some other source of information.

There are of course other sources of dynamic information that could help us know where we are within the week: cues in our current environment and memory for the most recent day name we heard. But unlike the fading of memories, neither of these sources has much to do with weekend-referring thoughts, and they seem more to be alternatives to the use of landmarks. I can see no way out of this problem with the forward-looking part of the landmark hypothesis other than restating the hypothesis in a weaker form. The essence of a temporal landmark explanation is that we know, in some sense, that yesterday was Sunday before we know that today is Monday or that we know that tomorrow is Saturday before we know that today is Friday. We have seen that knowing that tomorrow is Saturday cannot be the ultimate source of our orientation on Friday. However, it may be a particularly salient source of information during our actual attempt to identify the day when asked. This could be true if we had needed some general sense of orientation earlier in the day (for example, to figure out how much longer we need to continue working), and this led us to think more frequently about the weekend. These weekend-referring thoughts might then be among the first to come to mind when someone stops us and asks, "What day is today?"

Representations of the Days
So far we have been attempting to explain the ease of identifying days near the weekend (point 1 in the list) in terms of dynamic sources of information, such as changing thoughts or a changing environment.

Surprisingly, however, an important contributor to the effect turns out to be a static source of information, our knowledge of the characteristics of individual days of the week. This source of information cannot be separated from dynamic sources when we ask the normal version of the question, What day is today? But in one of the studies we have been examining, Asher Koriat, Baruch Fischhoff, and Ofra Razel used questions that can disentangle the two. Their subjects, Jewish students in Israel, responded to a series of true-false statements (*The sun rises in the east; Oranges are blue;* and so forth), the last one of which was *Today is* ———. On each of the six testing days (Sunday through Friday), the blank was filled by each of the seven days of the week for one-seventh of the subjects. This means that on any given day, one-seventh of the subjects should have pressed the "true" button (when the real "today" was given), and the rest should have pressed the "false" button (when some other day was given). The first kind of question is similar to normal temporal orientation questions, and the results showed the usual pattern summarized in point 1. However, subjects who received the other questions were effectively being asked to consider some day it *might* be and then to rule it out.

The results for ruling out incorrect days (described in point 5 of the list and depicted in figure 5.2) mimic the pattern for identifying "today" (point 1 and figure 5.1). Incorrect days are easier to reject if they

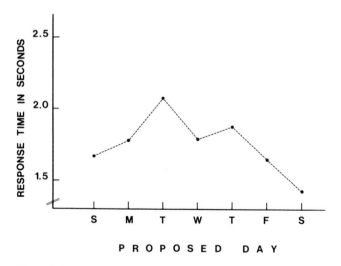

Figure 5.2
The time taken by Israeli students to rule out different proposed days when they were incorrect (Source: Koriat, Fischhoff, and Razel 1976)

are weekend days or days near the weekend than if they are midweek days. For example, it is easier to rule out Saturday than Tuesday, even though both are equally wrong.

Why should it be easier to determine that today is not Saturday than to determine that today is not Tuesday? At least part of the answer must lie in subjects' enduring representations of *Saturday* and *Tuesday* because we get the same result on Sunday, Monday, Wednesday, Thursday, and Friday. The information associated with *Saturday* in memory must be more distinctive than that associated with *Tuesday*, a fact that makes good sense given Saturday's special qualities as the Sabbath, a day off from work, and a day for socializing. Israeli students' representations of *Tuesday* probably include fewer characteristics, at least fewer that could distinguish Tuesday from Sunday, Monday, Wednesday, and Thursday.

Almost certainly, determining the present day involves some sort of matching between what one knows about "today" and one's enduring representations of the different days of the week. Days that have distinctive characteristics are easy to recognize when they occur (point 1) and to reject on other days (point 5). This is our first clear evidence that static information contributes to the process of temporal orientation. Quite apart from what day it happens to be now, we know what a Saturday and, to a lesser extent perhaps, what a Tuesday are supposed to be like. The study doesn't tell us what specific forms these representations take, but in chapter 4 we saw that networks of associations are well suited for capturing the *meaning* of time elements like days of the week.

"Approximate" Orientation

One might think that temporal orientation is an all-or-none affair: We either know exactly where we are or have no idea at all. But two of the findings of these studies show that we can be approximately oriented (see point 6 in the list). The first, stated a bit more precisely than in the list, is that it takes more *time* to rule out the days preceding and succeeding the testing day than more distant days. For example, if subjects are tested on a Tuesday, they will press the "false" button sooner if *Friday* is flashed on the screen than if *Monday* or *Wednesday* is presented. Apparently there is some brief period of time (about one-tenth of a second) during which subjects know roughly where they are within the week without yet being able to pin down the day exactly. During this time they can reject distant days, but are not yet sure which of the days near their true location is correct. The second finding is that when subjects actually give wrong answers to the question, What day is today? (which happened about 10 percent of the time or less in these studies), they usually give the previous or following day rather than more distant days.

The imprecision shown in these brief delays and occasional errors is not very important from a practical point of view, but it does provide some intriguing clues about the processes that lead to temporal orientation within the week. It seems that on many days of the week, there are two stages involved in determining one's location:[5] During the first stage we reach a rough sense of the present day, and during the second we determine the day more precisely. It is particularly important to consider what it means to have a rough sense of the day. There are two fundamentally different ways in which we can know the approximate day: The first is that we come up with a kind of short list of candidate days (for example, *Today might be a Tuesday or a Wednesday or a Monday*). The second is that we reach some sense of our location within the week without yet assigning day names (*It is the middle of the week*).

These two ways of characterizing the approximate knowledge imply quite different ways of knowing where we are in time. The method of considering candidate days is really just a stage in the matching process discussed in the preceding section: We compare what we know about "today" with our representations of the various days of the week. As we begin to search for temporally relevant information, we come up with some clues that fit our representations of several different days of the week. For example, a student considers that she is on campus, hasn't thought much about the weekend recently, and is on her way to a class. At this point the candidate days most resonant in her awareness are Tuesday, Wednesday, and Thursday. Only later does she think of a Tuesday-Thursday class that did not meet this morning, and Wednesday becomes the clearest label. (This narrative of course makes the process sound much more deliberative than a one- to two-second process could possibly be.)

This explanation of approximate orientation is supported by one of the findings from the study by Koriat, Fischhoff, and Razel. The first part of point 6 in the list is actually only apparent on Monday, Tuesday, and Wednesday: Only on these days do near days clearly take more time to rule out than far days. This makes sense if we consider that, for the Israeli students in this study, these days have the most in common with their yesterdays and tomorrows. On Sunday, Thursday, and Friday, either the "yesterday" or the "tomorrow" is a particularly distinct day within the week, one which would share fewer features with these "todays." Therefore, when the subjects are presented with one of these distinct yesterdays or tomorrows, they can just as easily rule it out as a more distant day.

The second way of describing the initial, relatively imprecise stage of temporal orientation is to say that one's approximate *location* within the week is known. Quite apart from having one or more day names accessible to consciousness, we might have a rough impression of our current position within the calendar week, an impression that can then be used to evaluate proposed day names or come up with to-day's name. This would be especially likely if there were some representation of our position that we occasionally activated and updated and could call up when someone asks us about "today." Two questions are immediately raised: Why should we bother repeatedly activating and updating a representation when we are so seldom asked to identify the day? and What is the nature of the representations?

When one thinks about it, temporal orientation probably occurs over and over again in the course of a normal day, not just when someone asks us what day today is. We orient when we plan our work, keep appointments, and turn on the television at the right time to see our favorite shows. To organize our time and synchronize our activities with social patterns, we need to know our present position relative to other reference points; in effect we need to build bridges to past and future events. Each time we require this sort of information, we may actually construct a representation of the relative times. Recently used representations may be especially easy to activate and may be the vehicle that provides an initial, rough impression when someone asks us the day.

The second question is more difficult to answer because there are no studies on the types of representations that people use when orienting. (The one-shot nature of temporal orientation makes this very difficult to study.) One possibility, though, is that we construct images of our position within the week. This is an attractive possibility because, as we saw in chapter 4, images are efficient ways of representing relative times of occurrence. If I want to understand my current location relative to a weekend party or a Thursday deadline for a report, imagery may be a particularly helpful medium.

Two kinds of evidence are consistent with the more general hypothesis that approximate orientation is based on a sense of *location* within the week. One is that when subjects err in identifying the day, they are far more likely to give a day that is earlier than a day that is later in the calendar week.[6] This finding is not easily explained by a matching hypothesis: Why should present cues provide a better match to the representations of earlier than later days of the week?

Errors based on shared characteristics might be expected to spread equally in both temporal directions and in fact should not show any restrictions based on what happens to be one calendar week or another. On the other hand, if we obtain a rough sense of what today is by referring to the most recently activated representation, it may sometimes be a little out of date (resulting in past errors), but is apt to give us the correct calendar week.

The second kind of evidence is similar in nature.[7] Recall that subjects take longer to reject incorrect near days than incorrect far days (point 6). I haven't said anything yet about how distance between days is calculated to make this distinction. In principle we could calculate Saturday and Sunday to be either one or six days apart, Monday and Friday to be either three or four days apart, and so forth. Because there is no absolute rule for knowing which method is correct, one might simply plot the relation between response time and distance for each of several ways of dividing the week and see which division gives the clearest pattern. It turns out that the best division for Koriat, Fischhoff, and Razel's Israeli subjects was between Saturday and Sunday (that is, treating this pair as six days rather than one day apart). When this division is used, there is a nearly smooth curve showing faster responses with greater separations (see figure 5.3). This result indicates that the *psychological distance* between two days—

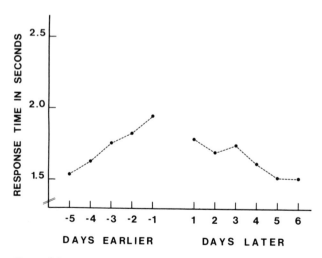

Figure 5.3
The time taken by Israeli students to rule out incorrect days as a function of their distance from the testing day. Distances are reckoned as number of days earlier or later in a calendar week running from Sunday to Saturday. (Source: Koriat, Fischhoff, and Razel 1976)

the ease with which one of them can be ruled out as a candidate for the other—is determined by their location within the conventional calendar week. If this is so, it would imply that the rapid rejection of far days and the slower evaluation of near days is based on impressions of their *location* within some framework.

The two ways of explaining approximate orientation are each consistent with some but not all of the available evidence. The method of considering candidate days accounts for day-to-day differences in the time needed to rule out near versus far days, but cannot easily explain the predominance of past days among errors or the influences of different days' locations within the calendar week framework. The location method has the reverse pattern of strengths and weaknesses. It may be that both sorts of processes go on simultaneously and generate somewhat different information about the present time. Considering candidate days may be better for finally identifying today's name, but the location method may be better for understanding where we are relative to other parts of the regular week structure. If this is true, the clear moral is that despite its rapidity, temporal orientation is anything but a simple process. We use many sources of information and many methods to determine our location in time.

Lessons from Temporal Disorientation

Sometimes we can learn a great deal about normal psychological processes by studying situations in which things go wrong. A good example is optical illusions, which are remarkably informative about the workings of everyday visual perception. In a similar way temporal *dis*orientation turns out to be a valuable source of information about our ability to know our place in time, and this is fortunate because there have been so few studies of normal orientation. Most of the cases of disorientation that I describe have not actually been studied, so I rely to a considerable extent on familiar examples.

The first example, however, is one that is happily unfamiliar to most of us: amnesia caused by brain damage.[8] There are many different kinds of organic damage that result in memory deficits, including accidents, strokes, chronic alcoholism, and even operations to correct other neurological problems. The specific nature of memory losses also varies from one syndrome to another, but a particularly common feature of amnesia is that it is selective. For example, patients often recall much of the general information that they acquired up until near the time of their brain damage (such as the names and faces of relatives, facts learned in school, and news events), but are deficient in their ability to store information encountered after the damage.

One such patient is especially interesting from the point of view of understanding temporal orientation.[9] H. M., as he is known in scientific publications, underwent an operation in 1953, at the age of twenty-seven, to reduce his epileptic seizures. Because of the severity of his condition, it was deemed necessary to remove portions of tissue from both hemispheres of his brain. The excised areas included parts of the hippocampus, a region we now know plays a crucial role in transferring new experiences into enduring memories. Unfortunately this surgical procedure had devastating effects on H. M.'s memory. Even when tested more than a decade after the operation, H. M. was largely unable to remember new events. For example, he could not describe the details of a job he had done every day for six months or even recognize a person he had met thirty minutes earlier, with whom he had conversed for more than five minutes. Given these striking deficits, one might expect H. M.'s memory losses to be more or less across the board. But this is not so. He recalled events through his early twenties, had a good vocabulary, and achieved a greater-than-average score on an I.Q. test (which included definitions, arithmetic, and other kinds of general knowledge). In fact H. M. was even able to remember random lists of numbers for several seconds after they were presented, showing that his short-term memory was largely intact. His pattern of strengths and weaknesses shows that H. M. had both short-term memory and long-term memory for information acquired well before the operation, but that little new information could be transferred into long-term memory.

Alongside his memory problems H. M. was disoriented in space and time. During the several-day testing period when he was living in a hospital, H. M. would ring the night nurse and ask where he was and how he got to be there. He always underestimated his age and, even though he tried to use the weather as a cue to the season, could "only make wild guesses as to the date."[10] H. M.'s temporal disorientation is significant for our purposes because of the combination of abilities he possessed and lacked. First, it tells us that having a rich store of what we have called stable information about time is insufficient in itself to allow one to orient. Given his performance on tests of general knowledge, H. M. undoubtedly had a thorough understanding of the calendar system and must have known a great deal about the characteristics of different times of day, seasons, and so forth. He clearly tried to use some of this information, as the weather example illustrates, but, lacking adequate dynamic information, was unsuccessful in determining the present time. The same problems seem to show that cues in the present environment are generally insufficient for orienting in time.

What H. M. lacked most was a sense of the recent past. He was deprived of information about what the time or date was the last time he thought about it, what temporally regular events belong to the very recent past, and how much time had elapsed since landmarks such as the weekend or a holiday. These sorts of dynamic information must play a key part in normal temporal orientation or else the rest of us would be as disoriented as H. M.

Our next example of temporal disorientation is so obvious as to appear vacuous, but it actually reflects a kind of converse of H. M.'s problems: Young children are disoriented in time. If you ask a four-year-old to identify the day, date, or time of day, you are likely to get some random response or a bewildered look. Presumably four-year-olds have an intuitive sense of recency that is comparable to normal adults',[11] but, unlike H. M. and other adults, they lack much stable information about time. As we will see in the next chapter, young children do not have well-developed representations of conventional time systems and probably also lack a clear idea of what a Wednesday or a Saturday is supposed to be like. Their deficit then is in stable and not dynamic information. On the other hand somewhat older children often remember having heard that today is Wednesday, without yet being able to recite the days of the week, or know the days of the week, but cannot identify the current day. This again shows the necessity of both dynamic and stable knowledge to achieve a true sense of orientation.

From the point of view of temporal orientation, young children do have one thing in common with many patients suffering from brain damage (though parents may at times be aware of other similarities): Their lives are often relatively undifferentiated in time. To a large extent one day or month is like another. If temporal orientation requires the use of current activities and recent thoughts to update one's position in time, both young children and hospitalized patients may lack necessary dynamic information. The sociologist Eviatar Zerubavel[12] has given a number of other examples of disorientation that seem to reflect the same limitation. People who work seven days a week, new mothers, retirees, students studying for final exams, students who drop out of school, and unemployed workers "generally 'feel' the seven-day 'beat' somewhat less" than do those who work on more typical schedules. Irving Hallowell's disorientation during his sojourn with the Pekangikum Indians in Canada was really a similar but extreme case of being deprived of familiar, temporally differentiated patterns of activity.

But whereas Hallowell derived some pleasure from his "regression to temporal norms less elaborate than our own," temporal disorientation can often have a disquieting quality for people who remain in Western cultures. The aversive nature of temporal disorientation may be a reflection of the intimate connection between motivation and knowing our place in time. When we are disoriented, we often have a vague sense that we "should" be doing something, but are unsure what it is.

My final examples of temporal disorientation are apt to be the most familiar. Imagine that you have been sitting in a movie theater for the past two hours engrossed in a gripping drama, and you are now leaving your seat and heading for the exit.[13] If you can recall being in this situation, you may remember experiencing a brief period of spatial and temporal disorientation before you regain a sense of where you are and what time it is. A similar period of spatial and temporal disorientation often follows waking from a dream. (It is significant to note that H. M. described his everyday experience in just these terms, "like waking from a dream."[14]) A third example would be working intensively on some task and suddenly discovering that you are disoriented with respect to time of the day (often expressed as "losing track of the time"). These cases of disorientation are significant in two respects: First, they tell us that we are not always temporally oriented, and second, they show that it takes some interval of time to achieve a sense of temporal (and spatial) orientation again. Temporal orientation is clearly a process, and one that requires a certain quota of our limited amount of attention. If we are fully engaged by some demanding task or if we are wrapped up in a novel or film, we do not have the cognitive resources to maintain a sense of orientation. Once the resources are freed, we must begin the process of constructing our place in time.

Actually we could also explain the same phenomena by referring to the location hypothesis. According to this hypothesis, we often gain a rough impression of our temporal position by activating a recently used representation. When we have been engrossed for some period of time, there may be no recent, and therefore no easily accessible, representation to refer to. Having little to work with, we must engage in a lengthier-than-usual process of reorientation.

A final example of disorientation illustrates a point mentioned at the beginning of the chapter, but largely neglected until now—that we can be oriented on some time scales, but disoriented on others.

When students take examinations with time limits, they must concentrate on the content of the examination while still preserving a sense of where they are within the allotted time. We all know of disastrous failures to do these two things at once, but usually students maintain some idea of whether they are in the beginning, middle, or end of the examination period. However, this is not to say that they are oriented in any global sense. If you interrupted them, you would probably find them to be disoriented with respect to day of the week, time of day, or even season. Similarly students rushing to finish a term paper might have an all too acute sense of where they were relative to the due date, but lose track of the day of the week or hour. In a previous section we saw that it is possible to be *approximately*, yet not *precisely*, oriented. Here is yet another sense in which temporal orientation is not an all-or-none affair.

Constructing a Place in Time

More than other topics, temporal orientation illustrates the main theme of this book—that time, as we experience it, is a cognitive construction. As solid and autonomous as it sometimes seems, we must constantly build and rebuild the temporal world that surrounds us. Our sense of a position in time depends not only on our stable knowledge of the characteristics of particular times and of where the times fall relative to one another but also on our ability to exploit changing cues. The fluctuating contents of consciousness and a sense of the recent past provide clues to the present time, often in the form of forward-looking and backward-looking thoughts. Important clues are also provided by a temporally regular and differentiated environment. Orientation in time involves the construction and reactivation of representations of one's location relative to other times. These representations do not capture one's position on all time scales at once, may not always be detailed enough to know the exact time on any scale, and cannot take place at all unless we have an adequate measure of attention to spare. All of this shows that our sense of place in time is just as transient as our ever-changing environment. The temporal aura that envelops us is really a series of fragile constructions, assembled from the haphazard materials that we are able to find in our surroundings and in our consciousness.

Chapter 6

Development

The Child's Discovery of Time

Unlike philosophers infants do not worry about the nature of time. They lose no sleep over the anomalies of an ever-changing present, the infinite divisibility of moments, or, for that matter, whether some knowledge of time is innate. Yet infants grow up to be philosophers (of greater or lesser stature) and along the way acquire an impressive knowledge of the temporal structure of their environment. How does the newborn human, who does not even possess well-organized circadian rhythms and whose bursts of alert experience rapidly wax and wane, eventually become capable of constructing the elaborate edifice that is the adult's world of time? The developmental psychology of time is an attempt to answer such questions and, less obviously, to help us understand the structure of the edifice itself.

In this chapter we follow the growth of temporal awareness from infancy through adulthood and along the way accumulate an inventory of aspects of time that adults have mastered. We will see that the foundation of many concepts is already present in early childhood, but that the boundless and uniform time of adults is a gradual evolution.

Origins of the Awareness of Time

If we could somehow shed all that we had learned about the temporal structure of the world, what would our experience be like? Perhaps we would inhabit a dreamlike region, devoid of causal connections, of a past, present, and future, of a sense of place in time. The question arises when we contemplate the temporal experience of infants. Of course the mental exercise cannot answer the question. Neither does our imagination allow us to dispense with all that we have learned, nor can we recreate the mental states embodied in the immature brain. But it can help us to raise some of the right questions about the origins and evolution of temporal understanding in children.

As we have seen in preceding chapters, the environment is rich in temporal regularities, from very short to very long time scales. Adults are able to represent much of this information, but how do these representations arise? The starting point must be some awareness of temporal patterns, so a reasonable first question might be, At what age do children first detect temporal structure in their environment?

The answer is that even in the first months of life, the perceptual system is attuned to patterning in brief slices of time. Evidence for this conclusion comes from a small number of the recent explosion of studies on the perceptual capabilities of infants. Research on infant perception has addressed a wide range of questions, but by building upon a relatively few fundamental methods. Most are ways of telling us whether infants can discriminate one stimulus from another. For example, we can present stimulus A repeatedly until infants show little interest in looking at it, and then present stimulus B. If attention is then restored, we know that the infant can tell the two apart.

In studies of temporal pattern perception, researchers compare infants' responses to light or sound patterns that differ in their temporal characteristics. One such study shows especially early sensitivity to the time information in speechlike sounds. Peter Eimas and his colleagues[1] at Brown University were interested in determining whether very young infants can distinguish between elementary speech segments called phonemes. (*Pat* and *bat* differ by just one phoneme.) Their method was a version of the one just described: repeatedly presenting one sound and then seeing whether the infant detected the shift to a second, different sound. They found that such distinctions could be made by infants as young as one month of age, indicating an innate sensitivity to the phonetic building blocks of speech. For our purposes, though, it is important to note that some of the phoneme pairs that infants could distinguish differed by as little as 0.02 seconds between the beginning of two parts of the sounds (the unvoiced and voiced parts). This shows that even by the first weeks of life, humans possess a remarkable ability to perceive certain fine-scale differences in time.

Other studies have analyzed infants' sensitivity to the temporal patterns of sound sequences—what we would call rhythm. Adults of course are highly attuned to rhythmic sound patterns and easily notice the difference between the regular ticking of a clock and more erratic rhythms. This kind of sensitivity now appears to be present at an early age. Figure 6.1 shows three pairs of rhythmic structures that can be discriminated by infants in the first six months of life.[2] These figures should be read as alternating intervals of sound and silence,

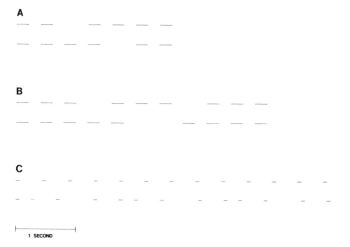

Figure 6.1
Three examples of rhythmic structures that can be discriminated by infants in the first six months of life

a bit like notes and rests of different lengths in music. For adults the locations of the longer intervals of silence determine how sounds are grouped together (for example 2–4 versus 4–2 in pair A). This sort of automatic grouping is evidently true for young infants as well. In one study changing the location of the silent interval (and thus the proximity of groups of sounds) by as little as 0.04 seconds enabled six-month-olds to perceive a difference between two sound sequences.[3]

This early sensitivity to the temporal properties of sound may be a special biological adaptation that allows infants to process information about speech. This leads one to wonder whether temporal patterning can be detected in other sensory modalities at such early ages. At least for vision infants at six months can discriminate stimuli that differ only in the frequency with which a pattern is flashed before them. One researcher showed that six-month-olds look for different amounts of time at checkerboards that flash two, four, or eight times per second.[4] Again we see that young infants are attuned to the differences between rhythmic time patterns.

So far I have described the early experience of time in terms of patterns organized within segments of a few seconds or less. To examine the awareness of structure on longer scales, we next consider the ability to sequence one's own actions and take account of the order of events that are witnessed. Here the most important evidence comes from a particularly fruitful meeting of the infant and the philosopher.

The Swiss philosopher and psychologist Jean Piaget, who created the modern study of cognitive development, was probably our best practitioner of finding the profound in the mundane. In pioneering studies of the 1920s, he made a series of observations of his own children during their first two years of life.[5] These observations are remarkable not only for their detail but for the far-reaching theoretical implications that Piaget drew from them. He sought to find the developmental origins of several fundamental kinds of knowledge, the best known being the recognition that objects continue to exist even when obscured from sight. One of the contents that Piaget considered was the knowledge of time.[6]

Piaget traced the infant's knowledge of time through a series of stages, spanning the period from birth to about one and a half years of age. During the first four months the only aspect of temporal order that can be seen in the infant's behavior is the very practical ordering of the components of such acts as closing one's hand around a rattle or bringing one's thumb to the mouth. There is no evidence for the awareness that either the infant's own acts or happenings in the environment have a regular order. But Piaget found that between about four months and eight months of age, infants begin producing actions that lead to interesting consequences. For example, his son learned to pull a chain that set in motion a rattle suspended above his crib. Piaget believed that this kind of behavior showed an elementary knowledge of a before-after relation, though it is also possible that his son simply associated pulling the chain and making the rattle dance about in some vague, atemporal sense.

The situation is clearer in the next two stages, between about eight months and eighteen months. Infants now interpose a "means" act before an "ends" act, for example, removing a barrier before grasping the toy that it hid. Now the infant seems to possess an appreciation of the importance of temporal order and thus to inhabit a less momentary world. Deliberate sequencing improves still further by the last stage, reached at about one and a half years. Piaget describes his daughter at twenty months arriving at a closed door holding a blade of grass in each hand. Realizing that she cannot both retain the blades of grass and turn the door knob, "she puts the grass on the floor, opens the door, picks up the grass again and enters."[7] The child has represented to herself more than a before-after relation; she has neatly planned a sequence of at least three acts to bring about a goal.

At this last stage children not only can plan an ordered set of actions but also can recall a sequence of events in which they played no part. A nice demonstration of this ability comes from a study of children's ability to search for hidden objects in a logical way. Robert Haake and Susan Somerville[8] showed nine- to eighteen-month-olds two scenarios in which an object was hidden in one of two locations. In each scenario the tester's hand (1) grasped and enclosed an object, (2) moved under a first cloth, (3) emerged and opened, (4) moved under a second cloth, and (5) emerged empty. In one version the hand could be seen to be empty in step 3 (that is, after it had emerged from the first cloth), and in the other it clearly held the object. Logic of course dictates that in the first version the hiding place must be cloth 1 and in the second version cloth 2. But this solution relies on the ability to reconstruct the temporal order of events. (Misordered "snapshots" of the information present at each location would not tell where the object must be.) The authors found that both fifteen- and eighteen-month-olds, but not younger children, showed a reliable tendency to look first in the correct location. We see that by about a year and a half, children are able to retain information about the temporal structure of event sequences that they witness.

Looking back over the first eighteen months, there seem to have been important changes in the scale of temporal experience. In the first month of life, infants detect structure in several-second chunks of sound or visual events. By the end of infancy children plan sequences of actions and remember sequences of events that take ten seconds or longer to complete. But even with the substantial changes of the first year and a half, there is still a large gap between the temporal awareness of the young child and the adult. The one- or two-year-old experiences isolated islands of time, not the boundless temporal framework in which we place ourselves. Children of this age must still adapt to long time patterns through biological rhythms of hunger and sleepiness and through the mediation of caretakers who structure the child's temporal environment.

Temporal Knowledge in Early Childhood

Until quite recently the period between about two and five years seemed a poor place to look for abstractions such as the notion of time. Perhaps it is not an overstatement to say that early childhood was a kind of wasteland for students of cognitive development, a relatively empty stretch between the impressive practical achievements of infancy and the widespread gains of the school years. This perception was due in part to our theories, especially Piaget's model of *pre*operational thought," corresponding to this age period, but also to the very real difficulties of administering standard testing procedures to young children. (Unlike infants they can escape our clutches!) Of course we were aware of the rapid pace of language development between about one and three years, but this seemed an isolated case, probably brought about by special maturational processes.

The change in our view of early childhood came when researchers began to formulate questions about this age period in much the same way as they had previously been asked of infancy. What is the easiest task we can devise that shows a given form of knowledge? What does spontaneous behavior tell us about the child's understanding? Using these general approaches, studies of the past decade have begun to fill the gap in our knowledge of the development of time concepts between infancy and middle childhood.

One line of research has substantially altered our view of the extent to which preschool children are able to represent the temporal structure of their environment. Until the late 1970s what was most impressive about young children's sequencing ability was their abysmal failure on tasks requiring them to reproduce the order of a set of events. For example, Piaget showed children a sequence of pictures that made a story, shuffled the pictures, and then asked the children to reconstruct the story.[9] He found that performance was very poor before about seven or eight years of age, with younger children "simply jumbl[ing] together a host of unrelated details . . ." By focusing on novel contents like stories, however, researchers managed to overlook the possibility that young children might know a great deal about the order of everyday event sequences. Such knowledge has turned out to be quite pervasive.

The earliest age at which temporally organized representations of event sequences have been demonstrated is twenty-four months. Two University of California psychologists, Barbara O'Connell and Anthony Gerard,[10] acted out three-event sequences for young children, and then encouraged them to imitate the actions. Some of the sequences were familiar (for example, a teddy bear getting into a tub, soaping himself up, and drying himself off), and others were reversed or made up of unrelated actions. Twenty-four-month-olds, but not twenty-month-olds, were able to imitate at above-chance levels. Their success was restricted to the familiar sequences that had been modeled in correct order, however, suggesting that they relied on enduring representations of these events' order and not on just a brief memory of what they saw in the experiment. Because the authors merely sampled a few event sequences likely to be familiar to nearly all children, it seems reasonable to suppose that individual two-year-olds in fact possess representations of the order of a large number of such events.

Memory for the order of familiar event sequences continues to improve during early childhood. O'Connell and Gerard's three-year-old subjects imitated longer segments of order than did the two-year-olds, but even at age three performance was less than perfect on their task. By four years, however, children's reconstructions of the order of common events are impressive indeed. Katherine Nelson,[11] of the City University of New York, and her colleagues have shown that four-year-olds are very accurate in describing the order of acts in dinner, lunch, and a trip to McDonald's. In response to quite general questions, such as "What happens when you ———?" children mention many component acts, usually in their true order, and even correct themselves when they happen to mention an event at an incorrect time in the sequence.[12] Table 6.1 gives examples of young children's event descriptions, including several cases of self-correction.

Table 6.1
Examples of Four-Year-Olds' Temporally Organized Event Descriptions

---

Birthday Party

Well, you get a cake and some ice cream and then some birthday [?] and then you get some clowns and then you get some paper hats, the animal hats, and then you sing "Happy Birthday to You," and then then then they give you some presents and then you play with them and then that's the end and then they go home and they do what they wanta.

You know what I do is, I just blow off the candles and eat it. And before I eat it, I just take out all the candles.

Making Cookies

My mommy puts chocolate chips inside the cookies. Then ya put 'em in the oven. Then we take them out, put them on the table and eat them.

Make the dough. And then you put it in the oven. But before you put it in the oven, you make the cookie shapes and then you put it in the oven. And then when the bell rings, you take out the cookies.

Restaurant

Sit down, and eat, eat supper. Pay, go home. First, buy a piece of cake and then go home. Go to bed. And then go to sleep.

Lunch at School

I eat lunch and after lunch I throw all my stuff away. First, somebody gets me lunch. Then I eat it and . . . somebody serves it to me and then I throw the stuff, the cup and the fork and the plate. And that's all.

Sources: Nelson 1978, Nelson and Gruendel 1981, French and Nelson 1981

Taken together, the imitation study and the work by Nelson and her colleagues show that young children possess representations of many activities in their lives and that temporal order is an intrinsic feature of these representations. Note also that the scale of temporally structured slices of time has increased substantially since infancy: Birthday parties, baking cookies, and restaurant meals (McDonald's notwithstanding) usually occupy an hour or more.

A final point about temporal order is that young children, like adults, use information about sequence to infer causal relations. We blame the rattling of our window panes on the thunder clap that sounded before, never on the truck that passed afterward. But until recently it was unclear whether young children could make similar inferences. Merry Bullock and Rochel Gelman[13] attempted to answer this question by showing children two potential "causes," one before and one after the "consequence," and asking them to choose which was responsible. The authors used the apparatus shown in figure 6.2. On a given trial a puppet dropped a marble down one runway, a jack-in-the-box popped up from the middle, and then a different puppet dropped a marble down the other runway. Children were asked to choose the ball that "made the jack come up." (The real cause was a remote-control foot pedal.) At each age from three through five years, most children chose the prior event. This study shows that young children possess a concept of priority that is tied to their understanding of the causal structure of events around them.

A second kind of temporal structure that influences the experience of young children is the distinction between the past, present, and future. Like order and the causal priority principle, the division between past, present, and future so deeply permeates our experience that it is hard to imagine its absence. Yet it is not an obvious feature of the environment itself, and many physicists have argued that the present has only a psychological, not an objective, existence. Perhaps the psychological roots of the past-present-future distinction lie in the early development of memory and a sense of anticipation of expected

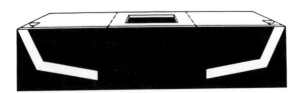

Figure 6.2
The apparatus used in Bullock and Gelman's experiment (Reprinted by permission of the Society for Research in Child Development, copyright 1979)

events. At some early stage infants or very young children may sense that there are both present and nonpresent happenings. By adulthood our appreciation of the past-present-future division is far richer. Not only do we conceive of an ever-changing present with the future vanishing into the past, but our experience is infused with knowledge of conventional time systems and of history, our ability to extrapolate the trajectory of our lives, and to impose order on our memories. We can even grasp the physicists' position that the three-part division of time is a characteristic of observers and not of reality. The temporal experience of young children now appears to fall somewhere between these two states of understanding, but it is really quite surprising how close three-year-olds are to the adult view.

The evidence for young children's awareness of the past-present-future division comes mainly from studies of the use and comprehension of tense. In a sense language provides a ready-made model of the three-part distinction. Children's task is to figure out what adults mean when they use different tenses and to learn how to map the distinctions onto their own experience. Several experiments have been conducted in which children are asked to describe anticipated events or events that have already occurred. These studies show the ability to use the correct tense by two-and-a-half- to three-year-old children.[14] If we look instead at children's spontaneous use of tense, we find even earlier success, particularly if we look at languages where tense forms are clear and consistent.

Though young children seem to share the basic division between past, present, and future, their sense of past and future probably differs markedly from our own. As we have seen, memories are seldom intrinsically ordered. To place them within a temporal framework, we usually exploit our knowledge of personal and social time patterns. But lacking both knowledge of long-scale patterns and of conventional frameworks themselves, young children undoubtedly experience a far less differentiated past. Probably past events can only be located within the islands of structure that we considered previously, without any appreciation of where the islands lie relative to one another. The future must be at least as unorganized because it lacks even the possibility of direct psychological information about distance from the present that trace strength or the elaborateness of the memory might provide. The future too can only be constructed once children grasp longer-scale structure.

The scale on which time is structured, however, does not remain static during early childhood. By four years of age children can order the different clusters of activities that make up their three hours at nursery school and even can demonstrate their knowledge of the order of four activities from waking to going to bed. This latter finding comes from several studies of children's understanding of the temporal order of daily activities.[15] In these studies children are given a set of cards depicting events such as waking, eating lunch, having dinner, and climbing into bed at night and are asked to place them in order. Most four-year-olds, but few three-year-olds, can accomplish this task. It is really quite striking that by about four years after birth, children's temporal horizon, their largest unit that is internally structured, takes in a span of as much as twelve hours.

One last feature of the temporal world of the young child deserves consideration, namely, duration. For adults events not only are ordered in time but also occupy particular amounts of time. But is there this same regularity in the young child's experience of the lengths of events? One way to address this question is to ask whether young children *perceive* time the way adults do. There is not a great deal of information about time perception in preschool children, but a few studies have shown that even four- and five-year-olds can learn to accurately reproduce intervals of about 3 to 15 seconds.[16] This would seem to indicate that their experiences of intervals of time are not completely malleable from moment to moment. On the other hand young children are probably especially vulnerable to some of the time distortions discussed previously, such as the interminable quality of an interval spent waiting for some desired event, like one's birthday or even dessert.

Another way to probe young children's experience of duration is to ask whether they are aware that particular events occupy characteristic amounts of time. Again it is possible to imagine that young children's experience of the passage of time would be so malleable that no reliable information would be stored about the usual duration of events. But this does not seem to be true. In one experiment even four-year-olds demonstrated some sense of which of a set of events (for example, drinking a glass of milk, watching a cartoon show, and going on a family car trip) were relatively long and which were relatively short.[17] This finding shows that knowledge about duration is another kind of temporal information that, alongside order, must be stored in the long-term memory representations of children of this age.

A third way to compare adults' and young children's experience of duration concerns the logical relation between order and duration. Here again Piaget's work has been very influential.[18] Most adults implicitly share Newton's belief that time is a uniform, all-encompassing flow, a single dimension along which any two events can be ordered and any two intervals compared. For example, we believe that there is only one correct answer to questions like Which of these two events occurred first? or Which event took more time? An alternative and startlingly different view would be that each event has its own local time, without any absolute framework of common reference. But as peculiar as it might seem, one could imagine how such a view might characterize the temporal world of the young child if representations at this age are entirely a matter of isolated islands of time.

To investigate the issue of the homogeneity of time, Piaget asked preschool and school-age children to observe pairs of events and then to combine temporal information from the two. For example, in one of his experiments two mechanical snails moved side by side across a table at different speeds. Both started and stopped simultaneously, but of course, given its greater speed, one ended up farther along the table. The children were then asked a series of questions about the successions and durations of the events they had witnessed. Did the snails start at the same time? Did they stop at the same time? Did the two move for the same amount of time? Children younger than seven or eight years were strongly influenced by the spatial characteristics of the situation. Thus the snail that traveled farther was often judged to have stopped later or to have traveled for more time. Interestingly many children were able to get the simultaneity of starting and stopping times right, but still failed to equate the durations.

Piaget believed that young children's errors on these tasks reflect a number of differences between their understanding of time and our own: First, time for them is not a single dimension that passes uniformly in all places. Local spatial information, such as the stopping place of the faster snail, outweighs the fact that both snails stopped at the same moment. Second, young children cannot logically relate succession to duration. Adults take it as obvious that two events that start and stop simultaneously must have identical duration. But as we saw, many children fail to make this inference. Third, time is bound up with space and speed for the young child, whereas adults (again, at least nonphysicists) consider the three to be separable dimensions.

Subsequent research has forced us to reconsider Piaget's conclusions. It is certainly clear from similar studies using pairs of moving objects[19] that the coordination of duration, speed, distance covered, and stopping place develops slowly, with errors common until at least ten years of age. But it also appears that our adherence to Piaget's methods has obscured some of the competence that young children possess and the real nature of their problems. Iris Levin[20] of Tel-Aviv University has found that even five-year-olds are able to correctly compare two durations on the basis of their starting and stopping times when the events do not consist of movements from place to place. One of her tasks involved comparing the times that two dolls sleep. The dolls would either go to sleep and wake up together; go to sleep in sequence, but wake up at the same time; or go to sleep simultaneously, but wake up one after the other. In each case children were asked whether both dolls slept for the same amount of time or one slept for a longer time. Levin also gave children similar problems, but using two moving objects, as in Piaget's snail experiment and most other studies of duration. She found that her youngest subjects, five-year-olds, were very accurate in judging duration on the sleeping doll task, but were only at about chance levels on the traditional moving object task.

These results show that preschool children can infer relative durations from information about the starting and stopping times. The results also show of course a certain degree of uniformity of time because the two events could be related to a common framework. The fact that children nonetheless failed the traditional moving object task, however, does seem to support Piaget's claim that there is an early propensity to confuse time with space and speed.[21]

This survey of the temporal knowledge of two- to five-year-olds has shown impressive competence where little might have been expected. By two years of age children are aware of the order of many common activities, and the scale of structured intervals increases so rapidly that by four years children know the order of the major events within the waking day. Three-year-olds use priority to establish causal connections between events. By about two and a half to three years of age, children develop a basic sense of the distinction between the past, present, and future. At least by four years of age, duration perception has developed well enough to allow children to consistently reproduce intervals of several seconds to 15 seconds. Three-year-olds have at least a rough idea of the amount of time taken by many common events, showing the early representation of duration. Finally, even five-year-olds are able to infer the relative duration of two events from their starting and stopping times, as long as distracting differences between the two events are removed. But five-year-olds still do not experience time in the same way that adults do. Young children are limited in the scale of time that can be considered and in their ability to construct a uniform past and future. As we will see, these limits diminish as children learn more about conventional time systems in the subsequent years.

*The Development of Temporal Knowledge in Middle Childhood
and Adolescence*

During infancy and early childhood one must look quite closely to find indications of temporal awareness. Clever methods and careful observations are needed to discover the nature of the young child's temporal world. But the situation changes rapidly during the school years and only in part because of the formal curriculum. Evidence of thinking about time is everywhere, as children learn about clocks, calendars, history, and time measurement and as they are expected to play an increasing role in organizing their own behavior in time.[22] Underlying these diverse achievements are two general trends that I use to guide consideration of the transition from the five-year-old's to the adult's understanding of time: The first trend is an increase in the number and scale of temporal structures represented (and in the nature of the mental representations themselves). The second is an increase in the uniformity of time, in the senses that it is measurable and unaffected by changes in clocks, time zones, or scale of measurement.

Between five and seven years of age, there is a quantum jump in the scale of temporal patterns that children recognize. Most six- to seven-year-olds, for example, are able to correctly order sets of four cards that represent seasons or holidays, showing that annual patterns are now within their grasp.[23] Children can order the days of the week and months of the year by about seven or eight years, and other weekly and annual school routines seem to be learned at about this time. Historical time becomes increasingly meaningful between about eight years and adolescence. This rapid growth in the number and scale of temporal patterns that can be conceptualized is probably due to the fact that children no longer need to abstract the patterns from raw experience. Memory and anticipation may allow younger children to fuse time representations out of the parts of familiar event sequences or a day's routine. However, they are unlikely bases for developing representations of much longer patterns. Unfortunately we know very little about how most representations of time structures develop, but two contents—days of the week and months of the year—have been studied in some detail.

We have seen that when adults reason about the order of months or days of the week, they rely mainly on two representational systems. The verbal list system enables them to move through the sequence one step at a time and is particularly useful for determining the exact separation between two elements. (For example, how many months is it from now until my August vacation?) The image system is especially suited to determining "where" two or more elements are relative to one another, when great precision is not important. (For example, is Labor Day or Thanksgiving my next holiday?) I have conducted several experiments that show that this two-system distinction applies not only to adults' problem solving but also to the development of children's representations.[24] Between about eight and twelve years, most children appear to rely only on the verbal list system for these two contents, but by mid- to late adolescence, the image system is also firmly in place.

Several lines of evidence support this age change: First, children younger than about fifteen years are generally much better at thinking about forward order of days or months than they are at thinking about backward order. This is exactly what one would expect if they rely exclusively on the verbal list system. Also preadolescents, but not adolescents, often move their lips while working on problems—even on tasks for which an image approach would be advantageous. This also supports the exclusive availability of the verbal list system. Finally, when children and adolescents were asked to tell how they solved problems that were designed to favor the image system, reports of saying the days or months predominated before about age fifteen, whereas older subjects usually described spatial forms of the days or months (like those presented in table 4.1).

These findings strongly suggest that children's first representations of the order of the days and months are chains of names. This is the way that adults usually teach these contents, and reciting is what adults expect when children are asked if they know the days or months. (In fact even adults seem to pass through a similar verbal list stage when learning the days or months in a new language. To get at the French word for Wednesday, I usually need to say *"lundi"* and *"mardi,"* for Monday and Tuesday, to myself.) The recitation method of learning the sequences works well for very long time patterns because the true scale being represented is quite irrelevant. Children are no more forced to abstract the order of days or months from the flux of experience than they are to abstract the order of counting numbers or letters of the alphabet. Symbols free the child from the limits of perception and memory.

The image system of course is also a powerful medium for representing patterns of different magnitudes. We can equally well construct images of neighborhood, town, and region, and likewise we can imagine daily, weekly, and annual temporal relations with equivalent ease. But adolescents' acquisition of image representations brings them a different advantage: By allowing them to conceptualize the temporal location of several different events at once, images, better than the verbal list system, permit them to see underlying patterns. This ability to hold frozen configurations of time in mind must be especially useful when we try out different orders in which past events may have happened, plan the best order and timing of future activities, and construct a view of where we are at the present moment.

The second major trend during middle childhood and adolescence is the increasing uniformity of time. As we have seen, young children are able to integrate information about the starts and stops of two different events to compare their durations. But this still leaves them a long way from adults' essentially Newtonian conception of time as a unitary, all-encompassing, homogeneous flow.

One important component of this seemingly esoteric view of time is the very practical belief that time can be measured, a belief that is not generally shared by young children. The evidence for this age difference comes from several experiments conducted by Piaget.[25] Piaget asked children to carry out actions, say, transferring small marbles from one container to another, at two different rates—first slowly then quickly. The tester clearly showed the children that both the fast and slow actions corresponded to the sand level falling a particular distance in a sand glass or the second hand moving a particular amount around the face of a stopwatch. Nonetheless children younger than about seven or eight years could not equate the intervals. In fact most insisted that the sand or second hand sped up or slowed down as their own actions changed speed! Before about nine years even children who assumed that a given clock worked at a constant speed had difficulty comparing equal intervals measured by an hourglass and stopwatch or two stopwatches whose hands moved at different speeds. If clocks speed up and slow down with our actions, and if two different clocks cannot be counted on to maintain their equality, then the measurement of time becomes rather pointless.

There is one exception, though, to the conclusion that children do not trust time measurement before eight or nine years. Six- and seven-year-olds, according to one experiment,[26] discover that their own rhythmic counting can help them accurately reproduce brief durations. Perhaps the counting strategy originates in children's games like hide-and-seek, where uniformity in rate and total count is an important part of fair play.

Another way of examining the growth of temporal homogeneity is to ask children whether changes in clocks and calendars affect "real" time. Students of time are fond of pointing out that our ancestors were not terribly clear about the distinction: When England finally adopted the Gregorian calendar in 1752 and the date of 3 September was changed to 14 September, rioting broke out among farmers concerned that the "lost" days would shorten the growing season. Nevertheless most contemporary Western adults understand the distinction, and it appears to be important by about nine to eleven years.[27] By these ages children understand that conventional time systems have some arbitrary features and that changing these features has no effect on natural durations such as one's age or the length of a day. For example, most nine-year-olds know that advancing the clock one hour for daylight saving time or flying to an earlier time zone does not affect how old they are. Eleven-year-olds, presented with the somewhat vexing possibility of changing to a "metric week" of ten days, reasoned that it would be a good idea to keep the day length constant.

This research, along with the studies of measurement, shows that during middle childhood time becomes a concept in and of itself, an abstraction freed from particular contents. Time is not a property of specific motions or clocks or even measuring systems but a more basic dimension that encompasses all events. It may have taken Western civilization until Galileo's and Newton's time to construct an abstract model of time, but children are able to acquire a reasonable semblance of this model before they reach adolescence.

We have seen that during childhood and adolescence there are marked gains in the scale and number of time structures that are represented, the flexibility with which they can be treated, and the uniformity of time itself. Given these impressive achievements, it may seem unappreciative to dwell on remaining limitations. But it is actually quite revealing to consider several temporal relations that continue to elude not only adolescents but most adults as well. One clear example is relativistic time, the historical successor to Newtonian time among physicists. Most of us have great difficulty imagining a world without absolute succession or simultaneity, a world in which durations expand and contract with changes in velocity.

Another more mundane illustration of our limited temporal understanding is the difficulty most adults seem to have in grasping the consequences of shifting to and from daylight saving time. Most of us need to be reminded semiannually whether mornings or evenings will be lighter or darker than they were before the shift. (One Cleveland newscaster urged listeners to put their porch lights on early in the morning after the autumn change to standard time to help children on their way to school. However, the change has the opposite effect, making mornings brighter!) I have studied this problem by asking college students to answer a series of questions about the effect of the spring shift on the clock time at which natural events, such as the sun rising or feeling hungry for lunch, will occur.[28] About 20 percent to 50 percent of students err on such questions. A more detailed perspective on the nature of their difficulties can be gotten by asking students to think aloud as they work through individual problems. Table 6.2 gives excerpts from several protocols in which errors occur. Many protocols seem to show the difficulty of coming up with a useful way of thinking about the critical aspects of the problems. A particularly common error is thinking of the change as being one-dimensional (for example, things in general are "later" or "earlier") rather than as a displacement between one reference system, clock times, and another, the sequence of natural events.[29] So, for example, there is confusion over whether the clock time of eating lunch is "later" than before the shift to daylight saving time or eating lunch is "later" with respect to the natural sequence, the times at which one becomes hungry. Very likely, attempts to solve these sorts of problems are so infrequent for most of us that adequate representations of the temporal relations never develop.

The daylight saving time system, time in relativity theory, and nu-

Table 6.2
Examples of Thinking-Aloud Reports in the Course of
Solving Daylight Saving Time Problems

In the spring we set clocks forward one hour for daylight saving time. What effect does this have on the clock time at which the sun rises?

If the sun rises . . . in the east . . . sets in the west, the sun rises. The clock would be one hour ahead . . . the sun, but the sun rises at the same time so it makes no difference.

Umm . . . it is just an hour earlier because the clock is set one hour ahead. Right? Yeah.

Sun rises . . . OK . . . You set the clock back you have to . . . the sun . . . let's see, it is lighter earlier, so the sun rises, objectively, an hour earlier, so because you have . . . right . . . because it is darker at night, so the sun rises objectively an hour earlier.

If you're used to eating at noon, are you likely to get hungry earlier, later, or at the same time according to the clock?

Initially it would be an hour earlier . . . No, wait a minute. If it's an hour later than you think it is, you'd get hungry an hour earlier.

Okay, if you're used to eating at noon, and you eat an hour later, let's see, because you're used to eating at noon you'll still get hungry at noon, even though it's an hour later. Lunch itself is an hour later, so around noon your stomach will start growling, and you'll sit there, and, oh God, you gotta wait another hour for lunch.

---

merous other specialized time structures—geological time, time of subatomic phenomena, time in the study of history, philosopher's tense logic—are mastered only when it is important for us to represent their information. The growth of the knowledge of time is a process of adaptation to an environment with particular temporal structures. We do not develop in the direction of ideal models of time, but rather build representations that capture relations that matter in our lives.

The growth of temporal awareness from infancy to adulthood is a change of impressive proportions. In early infancy this awareness is limited to the basic structuring of sensory events in brief "slices" of time, whereas by adolescence time has achieved great intricacy, uniformity, limitless scale, and in fact has become an object of contemplation itself. Of course we pay a price for this transformation: We lose the infant's freedom from the pressures and regimentation of time. What we gain, along with the power to adapt to a complex temporal environment, is the intellectual challenge of trying to understand the nature of time.

Chapter 7

Variations

Culture, Personality, Mental Illness

Being stuck as we are in our own skins, there is limitless cause to wonder about how other people's experiences are and are not like our own. Some of the most satisfying moments for any reader of literature come from recognizing in the characters feelings that had previously seemed unique to us. But there is also a great attraction to narratives that portray experiences very different from our own. These two facets of our fascination with other people's worlds are reflected in two kinds of psychologists—those who tend to be most interested in the common themes and those whose interests lie mainly in the variations. For most of this book we have asked the kinds of questions that engage the first kind of psychologist—questions about time perception, memory, orientation, and representation in people in general. This final chapter affords an opportunity to ask the second kind of question about time: How does the experience of time vary from person to person? I address three versions of the question, examining variation across cultures, patterns of personality, and categories of psychopathology. Our principal concern is discovering the different *dimensions* along which temporal experience varies.

Notions of Time in Other Cultures

The study of other cultures, like the study of children's development, is a useful tool for stepping outside a world we take for granted. Our examination of the process of development showed that adults' understanding of time is neither natural nor intuitive but is the result of a gradual, constructive process. Similarly the Western calendar and modern scientific notions of time are the products of a developmental process, in this case, historical. Since Galileo, Newton, and most rapidly since the industrial revolution, time has become an abstract, uniform, measurable dimension that stretches indefinitely into the past and the future. These attributes of our view of time can be seen in sharp relief when placed alongside the temporal concepts of traditional, non-Western cultures.

Time in Three Cultures
Time is no more mainstream a topic in anthropology than it is in cognitive psychology. Our knowledge about time in other cultures comes from the patient fieldwork and insightful analyses of a small number of researchers. Three studies are especially useful in illustrating the place of time in the lives of peoples who have had little contact with modern societies. No small number of cultures of course can be representative of the enormous variety of traditional societies, but the three that I describe are at least from different regions of the world: Africa, North America, and Asia.

The Mursi of Ethiopia.   When studied by D. Turton and C. Ruggles[1] in the 1970s, the Mursi were a group of less than 5,000 people living in southwestern Ethiopia. They live in a dry region surrounded by three rivers, largely isolated from the outside world. The Mursi make their living by a mixture of cattle herding and cultivation, both of which follow regular seasonal rhythms. Two plantings take place each year, in the spring and fall rainy seasons. During one of the intervening dry seasons, men and boys leave the riverside settlements for cattle camps in wooded grasslands, while women and girls stay behind to harvest sorghum. Then around March the two groups reunite at border zones, and in June and July they move together to cattle settlements.

The Mursi have a name for the yearly cycle, *bergu,* and divide the cycle in two separate ways: First, they have names for certain intervals of the year such as the main rains or the hottest part of the year ("the stomach of the sun"). Second, they refer to the "age" of the year in number of lunar cycles, from new moon to new moon. By about age twelve Mursi youth can recite an ordered list of twelve lunar cycles, each assigned a number and characterized by seasonal events. There are set verbal formulas for each cycle. For example, the first lunar cycle is described as the "subsidence of the Omo [river], movement into riverside cultivation areas."[2]

Because the solar year (which determines the timing of seasonal events like the rains) is between twelve and thirteen multiples of the lunar cycle, there is not a constant correspondence from year to year between one's position in a given lunar cycle and seasonal events. As a consequence there is some uncertainty and disagreement about exactly which lunar cycle one is currently in. If the Mursi are pressed, they will refer the questioner to "experts," but even the experts can disagree by one lunar cycle. In practice the disagreements are always solved retrospectively using seasonal events like the migration of animals or the rising position of the sun. People acknowledge that the last lunar cycle *must* have been one or the other after all. This degree of imprecision may be troubling to Westerners, but it does not pose any problem for the Mursi. For them the time is a matter of social consensus, which is always reached (even if retrospectively), rather than something external that must be measured with greater and greater precision.

There is one exception to reckoning the time of year by number of elapsed lunar cycles. The Mursi measure the progress of the Omo flood (and thus the appropriate time for planting) by observing the setting positions of four stars. Here is a case where precision is very important, and so they use a more reliable cue to the solar year. But this does not mean that the Mursi recognize stars as more accurate indicators of the "true" time than lunar cycles; stars are simply seen as useful for this one purpose. Again this strikes us as inconsistent: Why not measure time throughout the year in the most reliable way possible? But for the Mursi determining one's place in the annual cycle is a practical affair rather than a quest for the most accurate way to measure some autonomous entity, time.

It is sometimes argued that the true measurement of time is a modern concept and that traditional societies understand temporality only in terms of positions within daily, lunar, or annual cycles. But the Mursi clearly count repetitions. One example is their system of numbering lunar cycles from the start of the year. Other examples show their ability to measure duration in number of days or years. Although the Mursi do not normally know people's ages in years (and can exaggerate the number of *bergus* they have lived by a factor of two or three), Turton and Ruggles found that three men, working together, could figure out the age of a 25-year-old man. They did this by recalling significant events (for example, the clearing of a particular plot of land) for each intervening year and counting them off. Turton and Ruggles also noticed that one man knotted a cord around his ankle once a day, thus discovering that it was 72 days from the planting to the harvesting of sorghum. But they point out that in both of these cases, despite the considerable effort involved, the results were generally seen as insignificant and were probably soon forgotten. The measurability of duration through the iteration of units is clearly a part of the Mursi's understanding of time, but it is normally of little practical importance.

The Saultaux of Canada.   In 1932 Irving Hallowell[3] conducted field research among the Berens River Saultaux Indians, a group of about 900 hunters and fishers living east of Lake Winnepeg. Many of the people he studied lived up the Berens River, too far from the river mouth settlement to have had much contact with outsiders. Like the Mursi, the Saultaux's activities changed markedly from season to season. In the summer they congregated in riverside fishing settlements, returning to their hunting grounds for the fall and winter.

The Saultaux were highly attuned to the annual rotation of natural events. They identified twelve separate lunar cycles with seasonal activities and changes in the fauna and flora around them (Wild Rice Gathering Moon and Goose Moon, for example). However, as for the Mursi, the Saultaux's lunar cycles were not subordinated to annual solar events, so there were occasions for disputing what the current lunar month really is. Despite their sensitivity to the cycle of seasons, the year was seldom used as a unit by the Saultaux. The year was not quantified in number of days, and there was uncertainty about how many lunar cycles took place each year. Like the Mursi, people did not know their ages in years and ". . . there was little, if anything, that demanded calculation in annual units of time."[4] Age of course was very important to the Saultaux, as in all cultures, but it was viewed as a matter of categories ("fresh child" [birth to walking], "youth" [puberty to marriage], and so on) rather than a quantity.

The upriver Saultaux did not distinguish days of the week, but they did have names for relational days (the day before yesterday, yesterday, tomorrow, and the day after tomorrow). These could be used to specify when a ceremony should take place—ceremonies were not tightly tied to a calendar—but there was considerable latitude about the time of day that a ceremony would begin. The leader would start drumming not at a fixed time but when he was ready, and even singers who had agreed to participate might arrive anywhere from the morning to the afternoon, long after the drumming began. Precision within the daily cycle was of little concern to the Saultaux, and Hallowell found it difficult to arrange for his informants to come at a set time, so that, for example, the morning informant was finished before the afternoon one arrived. This is not to say that the Saultaux did not divide the day into parts. In fact they recognized numerous moments within the day, such as the time of morning when red light shines on the treetops and the time when the sun is halfway to setting. Instead their lack of punctuality seems to reflect the view that social occasions take place when people are ready, not when some point in time is reached.

As we have seen in the case of people's ages, time measurement was of little concern to the Saultaux. Nonetheless duration could be specified in number of cycles. The number of winters since some event or the number of nights a journey required were sometimes mentioned. It was also possible to describe a duration in terms of the points in time that begin and end it. In one of the Saultaux's myths, humor is expressed in the fact that the Great Turtle chased a mouse from when there was first snow on the ground until the waters were unfrozen again.

Commenting on the Saultaux notion of past time, Hallowell concludes that about 150 years is the limit of ". . . any genuine historic past."[5] Beyond that events happened "long ago" and belong to an undifferentiated, mythological past. The Saultaux refer to a time in the distant past when the earth was young and giant animals (the Great Snake, the Great Beaver) lived alongside mythical characters. But there is no sequence to the mythical events.

The Ainu of Sakhalin Island.   Well into the first half of this century, the Ainu inhabited the northwest coast of south Sakhalin Island. They obtained their food by fishing and gathering plants in the warmer parts of the year and hunting in the winter. The Ainu migrated from their inland hunting grounds to coastal fishing settlements at the start of the herring run in the spring and returned again in the winter. E. Ohnuki-Tierney[6] studied their traditional notions of time by interviewing a 72-year-old informant after the Japanese had resettled the Ainu on Hokkaido.

The most important annual division was between the winter and summer seasons. The Ainu recognized lunar cycles, but there seemed to be no interest in the number of lunar cycles in a year, and most cycles did not have names. The two exceptions—the month of marten trapping at the beginning of the winter and the month of the herring run in the spring—were not only named but anchored to particular times in the solar year. As for the Mursi and the Saultaux, the year cycle had a conventional starting point, in this case, the time of marten trapping.

The lunar cycle was seen as a unit, from the waxing crescent to the waning crescent, with the period during which the moon is invisible lying outside either adjacent month. Each cycle was divided into two halves, and the Ainu thought of the two in terms of contrasts. The first half, between the new moon and the full moon, was considered propitious and appropriate for religious ceremonies and migration. (The migration to the coast always took place during the first half of the herring run moon). The Ainu believed that the time between the full moon and the reappearance of the waxing crescent was a time of danger, rain, and snow.

The parts of the day were also invested with contrasting meanings. The daily cycle was divided into a "light day" and a "dark day," the former an appropriate time for humans to be active and the latter a time for demons and deities. The light day started with the barking of sled dogs around the time of dawn. The Ainu believed that dogs barked again at noon and at the end of the day. The morning was considered an appropriate time for religious preparations, and the afternoon was a time when the dead could be buried. It was taboo for humans to be outside at night. Like the Saultaux the Ainu had names for relational days (day before yesterday and the like), but did not have a weekly cycle.

The Ainu concept of the distant past also resembled the Saultaux's in that they believed in a time long ago when deities were numerous. The Ainu believed that the universe, like the human body, has a fixed lifespan, and that there have been multiple cycles of death and rebirth. However, there was little mention of cycles other than the present one. The more recent past was not divided into a sequence of years, nor were people aware of their ages in number of years. Instead, as for the Mursi and Saultaux, age was divided into present categories (children, younger adults, and older adults), and past years were recognized by coincident events (for example, a forest fire, abundant salmon, or a smallpox epidemic). In referring to the time of past events, the Ainu were more likely to mention recurring natural phenomena, like the first frost or the herring run, than coincident events unique to a particular year.

Constancy and Variation in Views of Time

When reading descriptions of other cultures, one's first impressions are of the novelty of their peoples' lives and ideas. In the case of time much of the novelty lies in the different calendars that are used by different societies. Calendars are indeed extremely varied from culture to culture,[7] but does this diversity imply variation in the way that time is conceived and experienced? Let us consider three ways of contrasting the experience of time in different cultures:

Abstract Time and Concrete Time. A number of aspects of the time concepts of the Mursi, Saultaux, and Ainu suggest that traditional cultures have a less "abstract" view of time than do modern, Western cultures. One aspect is the close connection traditional cultures make between temporal divisions and observable natural events, such as animal migration, river floods, or the lunar cycle. Our society uses many arbitrary units—such as the hour, second, and week—that are completely divorced from happenings in the natural environment. Second, the Mursi, Saultaux, and Ainu show little interest in the overall consistency of their time systems. The Mursi are untroubled by the fact that at any given time two people might disagree about which lunar cycle they are in, and the Saultaux and Ainu have no real coordination between lunar cycles and the solar year. In contrast the modern Western calendar is designed to correspond to the earth's revolution around the sun to a fraction of a second per year. Third, the Mursi, Saultaux, and Ainu do not name or number past years but rather think of past times in terms of coincident events, such as the clearing of a plot, a forest fire, or an epidemic. Finally, there are few occasions when the Mursi, Saultaux, or Ainu measure time, whereas Westerners are preoccupied with clocks, the amount of time remaining until their next appointment or the end of the work day, the number of minutes required to run a mile, and so forth. (Hallowell found that the only use the upriver Saultaux had for an alarm clock was making the bells ring.)

All of these features make the conceptions of time in traditional cultures appear less abstract than our own view, in which time is uniform, measurable, and stretches indefinitely into the past and future. But this concrete-abstract dichotomy becomes less convincing when we compare the traditional cultures to "psychological" time as described in the previous chapters, rather than to formal Western time systems. If times in traditional cultures are rooted in events and activities, so too is our means of temporal orientation. We find our position in time largely by considering current and recent activities that differ from one day to another. Similarly our ability to recall the time of past events often depends on our recollection of coincident occurrences that were significant in our personal lives or in our society. This method seems identical to the use of past landmarks in localizing an event in time by the Mursi, Saultaux, and Ainu. Finally, if members of traditional cultures are unconcerned with the meshing of time on different scales, so probably are most of us in our day-to-day thought. It seems that we use different representations of temporal structures on the scales of days, weeks, and years rather than relying on some grand, integrated representation. We also have found that orientation usually occurs on different scales, so we might have a clear sense of our position within the week but not a similar sense of position within the year. We use our refined, formal systems on occasion of course, but they do not seem to be a very important way of distinguishing our experience of time from the experience of people in traditional cultures.

Another problem with equating traditional time concepts with con-
creteness is that some traditional societies have extremely elaborate
ways of structuring time, ways that are not based on observable
events. The Balinese keep track of ten separate, concurrently running
week cycles of one to ten days each.[8] Each day is a member of a one-
day cycle (always the same), a two-day cycle, and so forth. Some
festivals occur on particular combinations of days from different week
cycles. For example, one festival is held every 210 days, based on the
coincidence of particular days from the five-, six-, and seven-day
weeks. Each day in each cycle is also significant in that its name is
associated with the propitiousness of particular activities. This system
is clearly not a description of natural cycles. It seems more a way of
creating patterns of meaning in time and using these patterns to
guide action.

Linear Time and Cyclic Time.   Another way in which traditional and
modern cultures are sometimes said to differ is in their cyclic versus
linear views of time. The time concepts of traditional societies reflect
their close ties to the rhythms of nature, whereas we think of time as
an endless continuum that encompasses all events. The Mursi, Saultaux, and Ainu time systems refer to recurrent events, and there is
nothing like the Western convention of numbering years sequentially.

The contrast between linear and cyclic time may be useful in em-
phasizing the great distance that most of us have moved away from
intimacy with natural fluctuations. However, the distinction is probably too formal and too global to accurately describe people's thought
in any culture. When pressed, the claim seems to be that people in
traditional cultures have no way of conceptualizing series of unique,
nonrecurrent events, and that people in modern cultures cannot ap-
preciate repetitive temporal patterns. This is clearly not the case. In
our discussion of memory for the time of past events, we saw that a
group of college employees remembered the time of an earthquake
better in *cyclic* time, by the time of day, than they did in *linear* time,
by the date or distance in the past. Conversely a group of Mursi men
were able to calculate another man's age by remembering unique
events for each year since his birth. Even the Balinese, who seem to
be fascinated with temporal cycles, refer to past times according to
singular events like the eruption of a volcano.[9] Another example of a
linear conception in traditional societies is the practice of naming
"age-sets"—all of the people who were initiated in a given year—after
a unique historical event. The Mbeere of central Kenya named the
age set of all men circumcised in a year in the 1920s after the coming
of the locusts.[10]

Attributing either a linear or cyclic view of time to a culture ignores the fact that time is understood by many representations. We have seen that we possess many representations of time patterns and that these representations include different kinds of temporal information, including order and recurrence. People of all cultures encounter a world that is made up of both unique and repetitive events, and all must form representations that capture significant patterns of both types.

Time Pressure and the Pace of Life.   One dimension along which cultures clearly vary is the extent to which people's lives are regulated in time. Undoubtedly members of all cultures form representations of environmental regularities and use them to achieve a sense of orientation and of what they should be doing now. But the frequency and precision of orientation and the pressure to be doing the right thing in time is undoubtedly greater in modern Western societies than in traditional cultures. This difference is evident to anthropologists like Hallowell, whose sense of needing to use their research time to best advantage runs squarely up against the view of the people they study that the right time for an event is when people are ready.

The degree to which people feel the press of time varies considerably even from one contemporary, large-scale society to another, as travelers often discover. Some of these differences have been studied by social psychologists. One pair of researchers selected comparable cities in each of six countries, Japan, Taiwan, Indonesia, Italy, England, and the United States.[11] In each city they measured the pace of life by three indices: the accuracy of clocks in downtown banks, the average walking speed of pedestrians, and the amount of time it took to purchase a stamp in a post office. Table 7.1 shows their results. Japan led the six countries in the precision of its clocks and in the indices of the pace of life, and Indonesia showed the least time pressure by nearly all of the measures. The other countries had about the same relative order on all three measures, suggesting that these three were all tapping aspects of a common dimension.

Another study found big city–small town differences within a single country, the United States.[12] In towns with populations of less than 8,000, the following took longer than in big cities like Baltimore, Chicago, and Philadelphia: (1) walking 100 feet after leaving a bank, (2) completing a postal transaction, (3) waiting for an attendant to arrive at one's car at a gas station, and (4) purchasing cigarettes in a drug store.

Table 7.1
Rank Order of Different Countries on Three Measures of Time Pressure

Country	Most Accurate Bank Clocks	Fastest Walking Speed	Fastest Post Office Speed
Japan	1	1	1
United States	2	3	2
England	4	2	3
Taiwan	3	5	4
Italy	5	4	6
Indonesia	6	6	5

Source: Levine and Wolff 1985

Comparing Cultures

We have seen a number of ways in which the experience of time is similar across cultures. Probably all cultures have conventional ways of describing temporal regularities, all tend to remember past times by coincident events, and all attend to both recurrent cycles and unique series. On the other hand modern societies rely more on arbitrary time markers and measurement, and their members are more likely to experience time as a kind of pressure to be punctual and to be busy.

Some of the differences between societies are most evident when people with different calendars or attitudes toward time come into contact. Adopting different calendars, as in the case of Christians and Moslems choosing sabbaths different from the Jews', can be a way of deliberately distancing groups, and conversely the international standardization of calendars reflects a desire of different nations to cooperate.[13] Contrasting attitudes toward time are especially noticeable when people from traditional and modern societies, different nations, or even small towns and large cities meet. The other group is usually perceived as slow and lackadaisical or brusque and prone to needless rushing. But even different people from the same community diverge in their experience of time.

Personality Differences in Attitudes toward Time

Time is such a fundamental aspect of human experience that it is perhaps not surprising that personality differences are manifested in attitudes toward time. The genetic and environmental forces that bring about individual differences in personality dimensions such as sociability, fearfulness, and energy levels also seem to cause us to experience time in different ways. In this section we consider the ways in which people in our own society differ in their attitudes toward time, and I describe some of the other attributes that seem to go along with these orientations.

The Dimensions of Difference
The first step in studying individual differences in any aspect of personality is to identify the main *dimensions* along which people vary. All of us have our own intuitive ideas about how people differ from one another and what general qualities we like and dislike in others. Psychologists who are especially interested in questions about individual differences have developed methods for identifying reliable dimensions of difference. One is a statistical technique called *factor analysis*. The basic approach is to start with a large number of measures that seem to have something to do with what you are interested in, assess a varied group of people on these measures, and then see whether there are clusters of measures that seem to go together. Going together means that people who tend to be high on one measure within a cluster also tend to be high on the others, whereas those who are low on one tend to be low on the others. By analogy the countries that were high on one measure of time pressure in table 7.1 were also high on the other measures as well—the three different measures seemed to tap aspects of the same thing. This kind of convergence between measures in research on personality gives us some indication that we are measuring a real dimension along which people vary.

Factor analysis has been used by Philip Zimbardo and his colleagues[14] to identify the main dimensions of people's attitudes toward the present and future. (In early studies the researchers had found that few of their subjects had a strong *past* orientation.) They began by writing a series of about seventy specific statements that seemed to reflect fundamental attitudes about the present or future. For example, the statement "I am able to resist temptations when I know there is work to be done" seemed to capture an important aspect of the ability to delay gratification until a later time. Next, groups of subjects were asked to fill out questionnaires made up of these statements, indicating the extent to which they believed that each statement applied to them. Finally, the researchers performed a factor analysis of the responses to the questionnaire to find out which groups of questions tended to fall together into clusters or "factors."

Zimbardo and his colleagues identified five main factors: two concerning the present, two concerning the future, and one pertaining to the experience of time pressure. The factors can be named and described by examining the particular statements that fall into each cluster. The first factor, called Future Task Perseverance, has to do with delaying rewards for later gain (table 7.2). The second future orientation factor, Future Planning, concerns planning and setting specific goals for the future. The present factors are Present Hedonism and Present Fatalism. Present Hedonism, as the name implies, concerns pleasures that one can experience without waiting for a future time. The Present Fatalism factor has more to do with the perception that one can do little to influence the future. The final factor, Time Pressure, relates to the amount of weight given to punctuality in oneself and others.

These factors should be interpreted as relatively distinct dimensions along which people vary. So knowing that people are high on the Future Task Perseverance factor doesn't tell much about where they are likely to fall on the other four factors. But it does imply that perseverance is a general attribute.

Group Differences in Attitudes toward Time
It is interesting just to know that these five factors are dimensions of some generality along which people in our society differ from one

Table 7.2
Sample Statements from Five Dimensions of Time Orientation

Future Task Perseverance
I am able to resist temptations when I know there is work to be done.
I keep working at a difficult, uninteresting task if I know it will get me ahead.

Future Planning
I believe a person's day should be planned ahead each morning.
I make lists of things I must do.

Present Hedonism
I take risks to put excitement in my life.
I get drunk at parties.

Present Fatalism
It seems to me that it doesn't make sense to worry about the future since fate determines that whatever will be, will be.
I try to live one day at a time.

Time Pressure
It upsets me to be late for appointments.
I get irritated at people who keep me waiting when we've agreed to meet at a given time.

Source: Zimbardo, personal communication

ost of Melges's hypotheses about the role of time in schizo-
nic symptoms must rely for now on self-reports and clinical de-
tions.[22] However, there is experimental evidence for one of his
rvations, that schizophrenics experience a racing of inner events
that outer time appears to pass slowly as a consequence. A num-
of researchers have compared the time estimates of schizophrenic
ients to those of control groups.[23] The general finding is that schiz-
renics give longer-than-normal verbal estimates of an interval that
presented to them and give shorter-than-normal productions of an
erval specified in time units. Both of these findings are consistent
th the interpretation that external time seems to pass slowly rela-
e to internal time, as are subjective reports like the one at the be-
nning of this section.

Why should schizophrenic patients experience external time as
assing slowly? Perhaps, as suggested in the schizophrenic's report
f a psychotic episode, the increased rate of inner experiences is re-
ponsible. According to the cognitive theories of time perception discussed previously, we gauge the amount of time that has passed by
assessing the number of internal and external changes that have been
registered. When thinking is disorganized and ideas leap from one to
another, there is probably a strong impression that a large number of
"units" of thought are passing through consciousness. This results in
the impression "that much more than usual happened per minute of
external time."

The Experience of Time in Depression

Clinical depression is a persistent state of sadness, hopelessness, diminished energy, and loss of interest in activities that used to be rewarding. Depression, like schizophrenia, can result from genetically
caused biochemical imbalances in the brain, some of which seem to
interfere with the circadian timing system.[24] But it is believed that
thwarting life experiences can also contribute to the disorder. Frederick Melges[25] suggested that a central feature in depressive symptoms is a ". . . foreshorten[ing] and constrict[ing] of future time
perspective . . ." Either mental slowing, which makes future-directed
actions difficult, or the loss of an important person or goal, on which
one's future seemed to depend, disrupt the normal forward-looking
quality so important to motivation. The future becomes clouded by
feelings of hopelessness ("My future seems dark to me." "I might as
well give up because I can't make things better for myself.") as patients find it difficult to work toward their goals or replace former
hopes that have been dashed. According to Melges, this loosened
connection to the future makes the passage of time seem slow.

another. One cannot help wondering, however, what sorts of people
are high or low in Future Planning, Present Hedonism, and so forth.
Several researchers have tried to relate these kinds of dimensions to
such attributes as age, social class, and success in school.[15]

In one study Alexander Gonzales and Philip Zimbardo asked the
readers of the magazine *Psychology Today* to fill out a questionnaire
made up of statements from the five time perspective factors and to
respond to several demographic items. They received more than
11,000 response, mostly from the United States, from people of varied age groups, occupations, and educational and income levels.
Gonzales and Zimbardo found that respondents under nineteen
years of age showed lower levels of Future Task Perseverance, Future
Planning, and Time Pressure than did older age groups. On the other
hand this youngest group was the highest on Present Hedonism,
and, along with the over-sixty group, Present Fatalism.

Income was strongly related to temporal attitudes. People with the
lowest incomes showed the highest levels of Present Hedonism and
Present Fatalism, whereas the high-income respondents believed
most strongly that the future statements were characteristic of them.
This same pattern was found when people were classified by occupations rather than income. Professionals and white collar workers
generally showed higher levels of future orientation and lower levels
of present orientation than did semiskilled and unskilled workers.
Other studies have shown higher levels of future orientation in students who have a clearer commitment to a particular occupation, a
clearer sense of their political and religious beliefs, who receive
higher grades, and—not surprisingly—who begin studying for a test
earlier than the night before it is scheduled. Perseverance and planning are clearly associated with higher levels of achievement in our
society, whereas a sense of the futility of trying to influence the future
and a greater commitment to short-term rewards are characteristic of
poorer people.

One of the five time attitude dimensions is particularly notable because it links the study of other cultures, the study of personality,
and the final topic of this chapter—time and disorders. We have seen
that traditional and modern cultures differ in the extent to which time
is experienced as a source of pressure. Gonzales and Zimbardo's
study further shows that individuals in the same society differ on this
dimension. But there is also evidence that a particular group—people
at risk for coronary heart disease—are especially likely to show an
obsession with punctuality, speed, and not wasting time.

The type A behavior pattern has become widely known since the
1960s, when research showed that people who possess this cluster of

personality attributes have elevated rates of heart disease. Type A people are hard-driving, competitive, angry, and show a sense of time urgency. (People who do not show these attributes are called type B.) One researcher has given the following examples of time urgency when driving: extreme impatience with slower drivers, changing lanes in traffic to gain a short distance, and carefully watching for the traffic light in the other direction to turn yellow so that one is ready when one's own light turns green.[16]

Several studies have investigated the temporal experience and behavior of people who report type A attributes on a questionnaire.[17] Type A students arrive earlier for experiments than type B students, overestimate the amount of time spent on a task—a given interval seems longer to them than to type B students—and work rapidly on a task even when there are no instructions to do so. Type B students will work just as fast when given a deadline, but type A subjects provide their own time pressure whether or not it is needed.

Type A people tend to be high achievers in their professions, so one might simply view the risk of heart disease as the price one pays for success. But the hallmark of this pattern is not so much the amount of energy that goes into one's work as the failure to differentiate between occasions when rushing is necessary and times when a more moderate pace is just fine. In a similar vein Gonzales and Zimbardo have argued that the future orientation that is essential for material success in a technological society is limiting when applied to one's personal life.[18] Zimbardo described his own experience of time:[19]

> As a poor kid in the Bronx, I grew up with everyone being present-oriented. My father would be out of work, but relatives would drop by and they would take out a bottle of wine and a mandolin . . . [When we went to college, this was replaced by a new orientation:] I was learning from my teachers at school to delay gratification for later rewards. I was becoming a future-oriented person . . . [Later in his career:] I got obsessed with the future. I had no time for my wife, my friends. If someone dropped by, I'd see it as an imposition rather than a pleasure.

Problems with time urgency and future orientation seem to develop when they are unremitting attitudes, when one fails to differentiate the times for rushing or deferring gratification from times to relax and enjoy the present moment. It is ironic that these two time orientations become problems only when coupled with another time problem— the failure to see one's life as divided into different occasions.

Time and Mental Illness

> [This disturbance of my time sense] was t⋯
> rebral activity in which inner experienc⋯
> greatly increased speed . . . that much n⋯
> pened per minute of external time. The r⋯
> effect of slow motion. . . . The speeding u⋯
> ences provided in this way an apparent slow⋯
> ternal world.

This description might have been written by a u⋯ ijuana, but it is actually the report of a schizophr⋯ psychotic episode.[20] Clearly mental illness is anot⋯ human variation that is associated with differences⋯ of time. A normal sense of time is such a fragile co⋯ tion and is so closely tied to one's sense of self that it⋯ disorders of thought and affect.

One researcher, Frederick Melges,[21] argued that disr⋯ chological time are a central feature of many kinds of⋯ ogy. In his view these disruptions not only are sym⋯ psychological disorders but can actually serve to per⋯ Two of the disorders in which Melges found a disturbed⋯ are schizophrenia and depression.

Time Disorders in Schizophrenia

Schizophrenia is a severe thought disorder affecting abou⋯ of the adult population. There are many forms of this i⋯ most are characterized by disorganized, illogical thought⋯ priate feelings, and in general losing touch with reality. M⋯ gued that schizophrenic symptoms are largely manifestati⋯ disorganized view of time. As the psychosis sets in, there is a⋯ breakdown of *sequential thinking*, the ability to place events int⋯ ingful sequences. Thoughts are juxtaposed chaotically rath⋯ being assigned to a place in time. The past, present, and futur⋯ become confused, with memories and future fantasies seem⋯ real as present sensations.

Melges believed that this lack of temporal order contribut⋯ many schizophrenic delusions. For example, confusing pre⋯ thoughts with the future can lead to feelings of clairvoyance or⋯ belief that the future is "rigged." Similarly the loss of a sense of ⋯ and future may result in a diminished sense of personal continuity⋯ feelings of "going to pieces." The missing gaps in a normal sequen⋯ of ideas can lead to paranoid inferences, such as the belief that "som⋯ body seems to steal my thoughts away."

These two temporal distortions—the perceived slowing of time and a feeling of alienation from the future—have been studied in research on depression. In one study hospitalized patients suffering from depression and a group of college students matched by age, sex, and education completed open-ended sentences and stories, which were then scored for past, present, and future reference.[26] The depressed group made more statements referring to the past than the control group made and were less likely to refer to the present and future. The lower levels of future reference are consistent with Melges's clinical observations that depressed patients experience less connection with the future.

The same study also supported the second of Melges's claims, that depressed patients experience a slowing in the passage of time. Responding to multiple-choice questions, the depressed group was more likely than the control group to report that time passes more slowly now than it used to and that when they discover that an hour has passed, it usually seems that more than an hour has gone by. In another study a group of depressed patients was tested shortly after admission to the hospital and again after discharge a month or two later.[27] About three-quarters of the patients reported slowing of the passage of time at the initial testing, whereas only about one in ten gave similar reports after recovery.

A number of researchers have tried to measure the experience of slowing more objectively, using standard time perception methods.[28] However, these studies have produced weak and contradictory findings. Sometimes the depressed groups underestimate time intervals, occasionally they overestimate them, but most often there are no differences between the groups. The studies actually reflect some confusion as to what the subjective slowing of time really means. It could mean that depressed people repeatedly overestimate the real amount of time that has passed (as the questionnaire studies suggest). This would lead to judgments of an elapsed interval that are too long and productions of some interval (say, 30 seconds) that are too short—the produced 20-second interval *seems* like 30. On the other hand depressed patients might mean that they are experiencing a kind of mental slowing. But, as we have seen, both cognitive theories and internal clock theories of time perception predict that a slow internal rate should be manifested in *under*estimates of external time and productions that are too long. Thus the sort of mental slowing that is sometimes attributed to depressed persons should actually lead to the perception that external time is passing too *rapidly*!

Yet a third possibility exists,[29] and at the moment it seems the most likely one: Depression has no reliable effect on the processes used to make objective evaluations of intervals of time. When depressed people tell us that time seems to be passing slowly, they may not really mean that they have noticed a disparity between their estimates of time intervals and the amount of time that has elapsed on the clock. Instead they may simply be expressing the feeling that their current unhappy state just seems to go on and on.

Whether this turns out to be the best explanation of the rate distortions that depressed people report, it is clear that the experience of time is intimately related to cognitive and emotional functioning. Just as certain temporal attitudes are correlated with problems in the normal range of personality, so too do we find disturbances of the rate of time and of past, present, and future time perspective in depression and schizophrenia. These studies of mental illness show us that time rate and orientation to the past, present, and future are fundamental dimensions along which people differ in their experience of time.

Conclusion

Throughout this book we have seen that time, from a psychological point of view, is many things. It is the flow of internal and external events, the framework for localizing memories, the patterns that we build into our representations, and the coordinates that we use for reckoning where we are in the present. In this chapter we have also seen that time is different things to different people. In some cultures it is mainly the rhythms of nature and the right moments to do things; in others, an elaborate system of divisions and a uniform, measurable quantity. For some people in our society, time is the tug of future rewards that makes present self-denial worthwhile. For others it is the short span of certainty within which pleasures should be seized. Finally, we have seen that in psychological disturbances time can be a form of chaos or an oppressive rate of change.

Time is a constructed dimension, and we must live in the temporal world we build. At best it is an efficient adaptation to the patterns of nature and culture, a structure that gives meaning to our activities and allows us to have many different facets to our lives. At worst, time is a form of tyranny. The more we can understand about the construction of temporal experience, the better we can fashion the world of time in which we want to live.

Notes

Chapter 2

1. Another commonly used estimation method avoids conventional units. Subjects use relative line lengths to represent the relative durations of intervals.
2. My main sources on circadian clocks are Aschoff 1984, Gallistel 1989, and Moore-Ede, Sulzman, and Fuller 1982.
3. Many shorter cycles, called ultradian rhythms, have also been observed, as have cycles on the scales longer than a day. See Moore-Ede et al. 1982.
4. Aschoff 1984, Fraisse 1973
5. Moore-Ede et al. 1982
6. Church 1984
7. Fraisse 1973
8. Aschoff 1985
9. The findings on the estimation of intervals shorter than one hour are contradictory (Aschoff 1985, Fraisse 1973).
10. In fact the nervous system is so rich in rhythmic phenomena that a vast array of potential timing mechanisms are available in the brain. Macar (1980 and personal communication) has proposed an alternative to the common view discussed in this section that there is a single, general-purpose biological clock. Instead she suggests that numerous neural networks may be involved in timing. A given network might gradually adjust to the duration of a particular, repeatedly occurring situation.
11. For example, Church 1984, Hoagland 1966, Treisman 1963
12. Judgments obtained by the third main method for studying time perception—the method of reproduction—should be unaffected by oscillator speed, as long as the speed is unchanged from the modeled interval to the reproduction.
13. Another kind of argument sometimes made for a time sense is that humans are capable of remarkably accurate time judgments even when in a nonconscious state. For example, some people claim to have an ability to "automatically" wake themselves at a preselected time. Although such an ability may exist, the evidence is far from conclusive, and it may be that some of the accurate wakings can be attributed to subjects rousing themselves relatively frequently. See Bell 1980, Brush 1930, Carlson, Feinberg, and Goodenough 1978, and Noble and Lundie 1974. A second situation in which a nonconscious time sense might be expected to reveal itself is under hypnosis. Here the evidence seems clear: Hypnotized subjects do not make more accurate duration judgments (Tebecis and Provins 1974).
14. Hoagland 1966

15. Alderson 1974, Baddeley 1966, Bell 1965, 1975, Bell and Provins 1963, Fox, Bradbury, Hampton, and Legg 1967, Green and Simpson 1977, Hancock 1984
16. Aronson, Silverstein, and Klee 1959
17. Clark, Hughes, and Nakashima 1970, Hicks, Gualtieri, Mayo, and Perez-Reyes 1984, Tinklenberg, Roth, and Koppell 1976
18. Frankenhaeuser 1959, Goldstone, Boardman, and Lhamon 1958, Goldstone and Kirkham 1968 (the previous two cited in Roberts 1983); see also Church 1984.
19. Fischer 1966, Frankenhaeuser 1959
20. Tinklenberg et al. 1976
21. Adams, Rosner, Hosick, and Clark 1971 (cited in Roberts 1983), Frankenhaeuser 1959
22. Fischer 1966
23. Church 1984
24. Fischer 1966
25. Hicks et al. 1984
26. For example, Frankenhaeuser 1959, Hicks et al. 1984; see also Ornstein 1969.
27. Pavlov 1960 (cited in Roberts 1983), Skinner 1956; see also Richelle and Lejenue 1980.
28. See, for example, Church 1984, Gallistel 1989, Richelle and Lejenue 1980, and Roberts 1983.
29. Meck and Church 1984 (cited in Church 1984)
30. For example, Davies 1977 (cited in Roberts 1983), Krebs and Kacelnik 1984, Lea and Dow 1984
31. Gill (described in Gallistel 1989); for an example of timing of much longer intervals, see Silver and Bittman 1984.
32. Brackbill, Fitzgerald, and Lintz 1967, DeCasper and Sigafoos 1983; see also Lewkowicz's (1989) review.
33. See Macar 1980.
34. Shaffer (1985) discusses models of timing in motor performance.
35. Particularly penetrating are analyses by Guyau (1890; English translation: Michon, Pouthas, and Jackson 1988) and James (1890; the quote that follows is from page 623).
36. I have reviewed about 70 experiments, most published since 1960. Additional sources can be found in Block 1980, Fraisse 1963, 1984, Hicks, Miller, and Kinsbourne 1976, Ornstein 1969, and Poynter 1989. My discussion is organized according to findings rather than theories because the different theories tend to address somewhat different issues, and none offers a comprehensive explanation for the range of reliable phenomena. The experiments cited were also designed to test a wide variety of hypotheses, and there are often several reasonable interpretations for their findings.
37. Allen 1980, Bakan 1955, Brown 1985, Burnside 1971, DeWolfe and Duncan 1959, Hicks, Miller, Gaes, and Bierman 1977, Hicks et al. 1976, McClain 1983, Miller, Hicks, and Willette 1978, Smith 1969, Wilsoncroft and Stone 1975, Zakay and Fallach 1984, Zakay, Nitzan, and Glicksohn 1983, Zakay (1989, experiment [E] 3). Only Michon (1965) appears to contradict this pattern in that subjects produced unusually short two-second productions in more demanding conditions, as if the intervals seemed longer. It is possible to attribute the shorter estimates with increasing processing difficulty in many of these experiments, including the one described, to the smaller number of answers produced. However, within-task comparisons have not shown a consistent relation between number of responses and duration estimates (see Smith 1969, Wilsoncroft and Stone 1975, and Zakay et al. 1983).

38. McClain (1983), Martin, Shumate, and Frauenfelder (1981), Miller and colleagues (1978), Ornstein (1969, E5), and Underwood and Swain (1973) support James's prediction, whereas Bakan (1955), Brown (1985), Vroon (1970), and Zakay and Fallach (1984, E3) contradict it. Hicks and colleagues (1976) failed to find a significant effect.

39. Frankenhaeuser 1959, E6, Goldstone and Lhamon 1976, Ornstein 1969, E1, Vroon 1970, E1 and E4, Zakay et al. 1983

40. Block, George, and Reed 1980, Brown 1985, Miller et al. 1978. Bakan (1955) failed to find a significant difference.

41. Joubert 1983, 1984, Lemlich 1975, Walker 1977

42. Cahoon and Edmonds 1980

43. Langer, Wapner, and Werner 1961

44. Edmonds, Cahoon, and Bridges 1981

45. DeWolfe and Duncan 1959, Hawkins and Tedford 1976, Quigley, Combs, and O'Leary 1984; but see Allen 1980 and Frankenhaeuser 1959, E11.

46. James 1890, p. 624

47. Block 1974, E2, Frankenhaeuser 1959, E4, Hicks et al. 1977, E2, Ornstein 1969, E7, Underwood 1975; but see McClain 1983, Martin et al. 1981, Mulligan and Schiffman 1979, Poynter 1983, and Predebon 1984.

48. Berg 1979, Mulligan and Schiffman 1979, Ornstein 1969, E8 and E9; but see Predebon 1984.

49. Mulligan and Schiffman 1979, E2. The quote is from page 419.

50. This point is consistent with the views of Block (1980) and Frankenhaeuser (1959).

51. Ornstein 1969, E6. Other effects of segmentation have been shown by Block (1974, E2), Frankenhaeuser (1959, E11), and Poynter (1983), but see Ornstein 1969, E3 and E4.

52. It has also been suggested that we turn on a special timer in prospective conditions. Though this is a logical possibility, I am unaware of any evidence that supports it.

53. Among the helpful discussions of cognitive theories of time perception are Block 1980, Fraisse 1963, Ornstein 1969, and Poynter 1989.

54. Frankenhaeuser 1959, p. 14, original italics

55. Again it should be noted that some theorists (for example, Thomas and Weaver 1975, Zakay et al. 1983) attribute attentional effects to distraction from the output of a special timer.

56. See Hicks et al. 1976, 1977 and Miller et al. 1978.

57. Fischer 1966

58. Guyau 1890 (Michon, Pouthas, and Jackson 1988), and see Fraisse 1963 and Frankenhaeuser 1959. The James (1890) quote is from page 625.

Chapter 3

1. Useful discussions of some of the models can be found in Estes 1985, Hintzman, Block, and Summers 1973, Linton 1975, Tzeng and Cotton 1980, and Underwood 1977.

2. Treisman 1963. Yntema and Trask (1963) also suggested time-tagging as a possible basis of time memory, but gave little detail about how this would work.

3. Murdock 1974. According to Hintzman and colleagues (1973), another version was advanced by Koffka (1935). See also Glenberg and Swanson 1986 for a model that makes similar predictions.

4. A version of the strength model was described a century ago by Guyau (1890).

More recent versions have been proposed by Hinrichs (1970) and Morton (1968). Some advocates of the strength model have acknowledged that people will use inferential methods (see the next model) if sufficient information is available (for example, Hinrichs and Buschke 1968).

5. The inference model is at least a century old (see Ribot 1901, first edition 1870). It has been proposed to explain memory for real-life events by Brown, Shevell, and Rips (1986), Friedman and Wilkins (1985), Lieury, Aiello, Lepreux, and Mellet (1980), Linton (1975), and Underwood (1977). Similar explanations have been applied to laboratory tasks by Anderson and Bower (1972), Estes (1985), Guenther and Linton (1975), Hintzman and colleagues (1973), and Tzeng, Lee, and Wetzel (1979).

6. This model was developed by Hintzman, Summers, and Block (1975; cited in Winograd and Solloway 1985) and Tzeng and Cotton (1980) and is also discussed by Winograd and Solloway (1985), who propose the term *reminding*.

7. See Mandler, Seegmiller, and Day 1977, Rothkopf 1971, and Schulman 1973, all cited in Brown et al. 1986.

8. See Godden and Baddeley 1975 and Smith 1979, both cited in Brown et al. 1986.

9. Wagenaar 1986

10. Sacks 1985, ch. 23. The quote is from page 188.

11. See Brown et al. 1985, 1986, Linton 1975, and Underwood 1977.

12. Studies of real-life events supporting this point include Baddeley, Lewis, and Nimmo-Smith 1978, Friedman and Wilkins 1985, Lieury, Caplain, Jacquet, and Jolivet 1979, Linton 1975, and Thompson 1982. Squire, Chase, and Slater (1975) have shown a similar phenomenon using relative recency judgments instead of dating, and Fuhrman and Wyer (1988) have found that it is easier to compare the order of life events when they are widely separated in time. Laboratory studies that show greater accuracy in judging the time of the most recent items include Brelsford, Freund, and Rundus 1967, Hinrichs and Buschke 1968, Hintzman et al. 1973, Peterson, Johnson, and Coatney 1969, Toglia and Kimble 1976, Underwood 1977, and Wells 1974.

13. See Baddeley et al. 1978, Lieury et al. 1979, Linton 1975, Ferguson and Martin 1983, and Thompson 1982.

14. This is sometimes called the *primacy effect* here as in recall studies. For support, see Hintzman and Block 1971, Hintzman et al. 1973, Guenther and Linton 1975, Peterson et al. 1969, Toglia and Kimble 1976, Tzeng 1976, Tzeng et al. 1979, and Underwood 1977.

15. The clearest evidence is from Hintzman and colleagues (1973). Underwood (1977) reported a similar finding.

16. It is possible to argue that long-term retrograde amnesia after brain damage is evidence for a kind of sequential temporal coding in the brain. For example, some amnesic persons have excellent recall of information acquired many years before their brain injury, but no memory for events closer to the time of their injury. This might be interpreted as the loss of part of the sequence. However, the selective preservation of information acquired long before the injury can also be explained by a slow process of consolidating memories, which is disrupted by the trauma (for example, Squire 1987). A clearer kind of neurological support for a temporal sequence model would be the selective loss of information from a particular interval of time well before the injury.

17. The method I describe is closest to that of Tzeng and colleagues (1979, E1), but similar conclusions can be drawn from Tzeng 1976, E2, and Flexser and Bower 1974, E1.

18. Brown et al. 1985, E3. A third knowledge-estimation group was tested, but their data add little to the interpretation.
19. Brown et al. 1985, E1
20. Of course thinking-aloud protocols are now extensively used, and Brown and colleagues (1986) use this as their main method. Erikson and Simon (1980) discuss how and when verbal reports should be used as evidence. Brown and colleagues' methods seem to meet these criteria.
21. See Baddeley et al. 1978, Brown et al. 1986, Ferguson and Martin 1983, Friedman 1987, Friedman and Wilkins 1985, Lieury et al. 1980, Linton 1975, and Thompson 1982.
22. The scale effects method was developed in collaboration with Arnold Wilkins of the Applied Psychology Unit of the Medical Research Council in Cambridge, England. There are two relevant studies: Friedman and Wilkins 1985 and Friedman 1987. The latter is the one described here.
23. Some support for this interpretation comes from the strategy reports of Underwood's subjects (1977, E4).
24. Support comes from Tzeng and Cotton (1980), Winograd and Solloway (1985), and Tzeng, Lee, and Wetzel (1979). Seemingly dissonant evidence is found in Fuhrman and Wyer's (1988, E2) study of judgments of the order of life events. Tzeng, Lee, and Wetzel (1979) point out that the reminding model (which Tzeng and his colleagues call the *study-phase retrieval* model) is compatible with versions of the inference model.
25. Tzeng and Cotton 1980, E1. I have not mentioned their control condition, which consisted of a list of unrelated words.
26. Winograd and Solloway (1985) also found above-chance judgments for unrelated pairs, and of course most of the other studies using word lists have not selected the words according to categories.
27. Belleza (1982) and Bjork (1978) discuss the related problem of *updating*, replacing old information with more current information.
28. Linton (1975) and Brown and colleagues (1985, 1986) also suggest that multiple approaches are used to determine the time of past events.
29. Friedman and Wilkins 1985
30. Underwood (1977, p. 1) reached a similar conclusion: ". . . our ability to identify points in time at which particular memories were established is very poorly developed."
31. In Brown and Kulik's (1977) study of "flashbulb memories" of assassinations, the place, affect, and informant were among the most frequently recalled items of information. Pillemer's (1984) study of memories of the 1981 assassination attempt on President Reagan also showed that place and informant were very frequently recalled. Pillemer suggests that affect was less memorable in his study because most respondents probably soon learned that the injuries were not serious.
32. The exceptions are the studies of scale effects: Friedman and Wilkins 1985 and Friedman 1987.

Chapter 4

1. For a discussion of the history of the idea of mental imagery, see Paivio 1971.
2. Hadamard (1945) gives examples from a variety of fields, as does Shepard (1978), who argues that imagery is especially suited to innovative thinking.
3. See Galton 1880, 1883.

4. The study was by Guilford (1926). The first quotation is the article title, and the second appears on page 423.
5. Oswald 1960, Werner and Kaplan 1963
6. Seymour 1980a, Schroeder 1980
7. The data in table 4.1 for time of day are averaged from Schroeder's studies 1 and 2. The remaining data are from Seymour, but Schroeder's results for time of the week are quite similar. Schroeder did not specify month or season for his time-of-year question, so the findings cannot be compared with Seymour's.
8. Among the many sources on imagery theory are Paivio 1971, 1986, Baddeley, Grant, Wight, and Thompson 1974, Kosslyn and Pomerantz 1977, and Shepard and Podgorny 1978.
9. Paivio 1978
10. These studies are reported in Friedman 1983, 1984, 1989. Several of the experiments in these publications also test alternative models. Seymour (1980a, b) has also conducted a number of experiments applying the analog approach to temporal contents, but he interprets his results in terms of a semantic model.
11. One nonbawdy mnemonic for the cranial nerves is, "On old Olympus's towering top, a Finn and German viewed some hops" (olfactory, optic, oculomotor, trochlear, trigeminal, abducens, facial, acoustic, glossopharyngeal, vagus, spinal accessory, hyperglossal).
12. But as Klahr, Chase, and Lovelace (1983) have shown, long lists like the alphabet are really comprised of a series of sublists, or *chunks*.
13. See Aiken and Williams 1973.
14. Friedman 1983, E4. See also Hamilton and Sanford 1978 and Lovelace, Powell, and Brooks 1973.
15. See Friedman 1983, E3 and E4 and Seymour 1980b, E3.
16. Friedman 1983, E3 and E4
17. Friedman 1983, E4, Seymour 1980a, E3
18. Seymour 1980b, E1. Friedman and Wilkins (1985) report the relative number of associations given to elements of several different scales. Months showed the greatest number of associations.
19. Robinson 1986, Osgood, May, and Miron 1975 (cited in Robinson 1986)
20. See, for example, Collins and Loftus 1975.
21. Of course the nature of the parcels of meaning is the subject of disagreement, and temporal terms such as *before, after, until,* and *at the same time* and the use of tense are likely to be especially difficult to analyze. Miller and Johnson-Laird (1976) and van Benthem (1985) discuss some of these complexities.

Chapter 5

1. Hallowell 1937, pp. 650–651. The text goes on to point out the relative ease with which Hallowell was able to adopt an alternative, less differentiated frame of reference that derived from the Pekangikum culture.
2. This definition is derived from Kuiper's (1978) definition of spatial orientation.
3. Koriat and Fischhoff 1974, Koriat, Fischhoff, and Razel 1976, Shanon 1979
4. Hallowell (1937) provides an example of the role of landmarks in the early differentiation of days of the week in a culture that did not traditionally make such a distinction. Those Pekangikum Indians who lived near the mouth of the Berens River in 1932 used a set of day names that revolved around cycles observed by missionaries and traders. Hallowell gives the following approximate equivalents: Sunday = praying day, Monday = cease praying day, Tuesday = two

days after praying day, Wednesday = half the week gone, Thursday = great half gone, Friday = approaching day, Saturday = flour day (reflecting the paying practices of the Hudson's Bay Company).

5. Two-stage models are described by Koriat and Fischhoff (1974) and Koriat, Fischhoff, and Razel (1976).

6. This finding is from Koriat and Fischhoff 1974. It should be pointed out that this overrepresentation of earlier days could be due to a preponderance of "yesterday" answers, and, because testing took place between 9:00 and 10:00 AM, "yesterday" thoughts may have been more compelling than "tomorrow" thoughts.

7. Koriat, Fischhoff, and Razel 1976

8. See Squire 1987.

9. Milner, Corkin, and Teuber 1968, Richards 1973. Problems with recency judgments in amnesia are also addressed by Hurst and Volpe (1982), Sanders and Warrington (1971), Squire (1982), and Squire, Nadel, and Slater (1981). Sacks (1985, ch. 2) provides a vivid description of temporal disorientation in a patient with amnesia induced by chronic alcoholism. Tulving (1985b) has identified another aspect of temporal disorientation in an amnesic patient he has studied, the inability to relate the present to personal events in the past or to future expectations. This man "knows units of time and their relations perfectly well" (1985b, p. 4), but suffers from a profound deficit that mainly affects "episodic memory" (see Tulving 1985a).

10. Milner et al. 1968, p. 216

11. The existing literature is very limited and somewhat contradictory. See Brown 1973, Mathews and Fozard 1970, and von Wright 1973

12. Zerubavel 1985. The quote is from page 136.

13. I am grateful to Alan Sunderland for suggesting this example.

14. Milner et al. 1968

Chapter 6

1. Eimas 1985, Eimas, Siqueland, Jusczyk, and Vigorito 1971

2. Figure 6.1 is based on studies by Demany, McKenzie, and Vurpillot (1977) and Morrongiello (1984). See also Morrongiello and Trehub 1987 and Lewkowicz's (1989) review.

3. Morrongiello 1984

4. Lewkowicz 1985. Similar discriminations can be made at even earlier ages (Lewkowicz 1989).

5. Piaget 1952, 1954

6. Piaget 1954

7. Piaget 1952; the quote is from page 339.

8. Haake and Somerville 1985

9. Piaget 1969; the quote is from page 272.

10. O'Connell and Gerard 1985

11. Nelson 1986

12. These examples also show young children's correct use of terms for temporal succession such as *before* and *after*. In other studies (Carni and French 1984, French and Nelson 1981, Friedman and Seely 1976, Stevenson and Pollitt 1987) children as young as three years of age have demonstrated comprehension of similar terms that express succession and simultaneity in unfamiliar tasks. These findings show that young children's experience of temporal order is not just the product of some automatic tendency of memory to record temporal se-

quences. Instead children as young as three years must understand the meaning of priority, posteriority, and simultaneity in some abstract sense.

13. Bullock and Gelman 1979
14. See Harner 1981, 1982, Weist 1989, and Weist, Wysocka, Witkowska-Stadnik, Buczowska, and Konieczna 1984
15. See W. Friedman 1977 and Muto 1982.
16. Crowder and Hohle 1970, E. Friedman 1977; and see Friedman 1978, Macar 1988, Macar and Grondin 1988, Pouthas 1985, and Pouthas and Jacquet 1987.
17. Friedman, in press, E3
18. Piaget 1969
19. For example, Acredolo, Adams, and Schmid 1984, Levin 1982, Montangero 1985, Siegler and Richards 1979
20. Levin 1977
21. Even this conclusion may need to be qualified in light of Levin's (1982) research. She found that young children confuse time not only with relevant dimensions, such as speed and space, but also with completely irrelevant cues, such as the relative brightness of a pair of light bulbs. This seems to reflect an early propensity to be misled by salient cues rather than a fundamental confusion of time, space, and speed. Spatial position may have a special potency, however, among the possible range of distracting cues.
22. See Friedman 1978.
23. W. Friedman 1977
24. Friedman 1986
25. Piaget 1969
26. Wilkening, Levin, and Druyan 1987
27. Friedman 1982
28. These studies are unpublished.
29. A useful way to demonstrate the underlying relation is to take two index cards and draw the following information on them: On the bottom of the first card, mark a point about one inch from the left side and label it *sun rises*. Make another point one inch from the right side and label it *sun sets*. Now place the second card below the first, and mark a row of clock times along its top from 6:00 AM to 8:00 PM. Line up 7:00 AM with *sun rises* on the top card and 7:00 PM with *sun sets*. Now assume it is spring, and we are switching from standard time to daylight saving time. In the spring we turn our clocks forward, (that is, we make the hour read one hour later). To simulate this change, slide the bottom card a little bit to the left, so that *sun sets* is now lined up with 8:00 PM. Any natural event within the top series (the sun rising, the sun at its zenith, and so forth) is simply displaced to a later clock time. The autumn change can be simulated simply by sliding the bottom card back to its original position. (Of course the correspondence between the two scales in this example is arbitrary and depends on time of year, latitude, and longitude.)

Chapter 7

1. Turton and Ruggles 1978
2. Turton and Ruggles 1978, p. 588
3. Hallowell 1937
4. Hallowell 1937, p. 665
5. Hallowell 1937, p. 667
6. Ohnuki-Tierney 1973

7. See Zerubavel 1981.
8. Howe 1981
9. Howe 1981
10. Glazier 1976 and personal communication
11. Levine and Wolff 1985. See also Levine, West, and Reis 1980.
12. Lowin, Hottes, Sandler, and Bornstein 1971
13. See Zerubavel 1985.
14. Gonzales and Zimbardo 1985, Zimbardo, personal communication, Zimbardo and Gonzales 1984
15. De Volder and Lens 1982, Rappaport, Enrich, and Wilson 1985, Gonzales and Zimbardo 1985, Zimbardo (described in Goleman 1986)
16. Wright 1988
17. Burnam, Pennebaker, and Glass 1975, Gastorf 1980, Yarnold and Grimm 1982; but see Retzlaff 1982.
18. Gonzales and Zimbardo 1985
19. Goleman 1986, p. 16
20. Coate 1964 (cited in Freedman 1974)
21. Melges 1982. The quotes are from pages 141–143. See also Melges 1988.
22. Actually Melges (1982) provides another kind of indirect evidence. He and his colleagues have demonstrated that schizophreniclike experiences and time distortions occur together when large doses of THC are administered to humans. Melges believed that a common mechanism may be the impairment of immediate memory.
23. Densen 1977, Tysk 1983, 1984b, Wahl and Seig 1980, and see Melges and Fougerousse 1966.
24. See Edlund 1987.
25. Melges 1982. The quotes are from pages 177 and 179.
26. Wyrick and Wyrick 1977. See also Dilling and Rabin 1967.
27. Mezey and Cohen 1961
28. A. Friedman 1964, Dilling and Rabin 1967, Melges and Fougerousse 1966, Mezey and Cohen 1961, Newman and Gaudiano 1984, Tysk 1984a, 1985, Wyrick and Wyrick 1977
29. See Hawkins, French, Crawford, and Enzle 1988.

References

Acredolo, C., Adams, A., and Schmid, J. (1984). On the understanding of the relationships between speed, duration, and distance. *Child Development, 55*, 2151–2159.

Adams, N., Rosner, B. S., Hosick, E. C., and Clark, D. L. (1971). Effect of anesthetic drugs on time production and alpha rhythm. *Perception and Psychophysics, 10*, 133–136.

Aiken, L. R., and Williams, E. N. (1973). Response times in adding and multiplying single-digit numbers. *Perceptual and Motor Skills, 37*, 3–13.

Alderson, M. J. (1974). Effect of increased body temperature on the perception of time. *Nursing Research, 23*, 42–49.

Allen, D. A. (1980). Filling time versus affective response to the activity that fills the time: Independent effects on time judgments? *Perceptual and Motor Skills, 51*, 723–727.

Anderson, J. R., and Bower, G. H. (1972). Recognition and retrieval processes in free recall. *Psychological Review, 79*, 97–123.

Aronson, H., Silverstein, A. B., and Klee, G. D. (1959). Influence of lysergic acid diethylamide (LSD-25) on subjective time. *Archives of General Psychiatry, 1*, 469–472.

Aschoff, J. (1984). Circadian timing. In J. Gibbon and L. Allen (Eds.), *Timing and Time Perception* (pp. 442–468). New York: New York Academy of Sciences.

Aschoff, J. (1985). On the perception of time during prolonged temporal isolation. *Human Neurobiology, 4*, 41–52.

Baddeley, A. D. (1966). Time estimation at reduced body temperature. *American Journal of Psychology, 79*, 475–479.

Baddeley, A. D., Grant, S., Wight, E., and Thompson, N. (1974). Imagery and visual working memory. In P. M. A. Rabbitt and S. Dornic (Eds.), *Attention and Performance, V*. London: Academic Press.

Baddeley, A. D., Lewis, V., and Nimmo-Smith, I. (1978). When did you last . . . ? In M. M. .Gruneberg and R. N. Sykes (Eds.), *Practical Aspects of Memory*. London: Academic Press.

Bakan, P. (1955). Effect of set and work speed on time estimation. *Perceptual and Motor Skills, 5*, 147–148.

Belleza, F. S. (1982). Updating memory using mnemonic devices. *Cognitive Psychology, 14*, 301–327.

Bell, C. R. (1965). Time estimation and increases in body temperature. *Journal of Experimental Psychology, 70*, 232–234.

Bell, C. R. (1975). Effects of lowered temperature on time estimation. *Quarterly Journal of Experimental Psychology, 27*, 531–538.

Bell, C. R. (1980). Awakening from sleep at a pre-set time. *Perceptual and Motor Skills,* *50,* 503–508.

Bell, C. R., and Provins, K. A. (1963). Relation between physiological responses to environmental heat and time judgments. *Journal of Experimental Psychology, 66,* 572–579.

Berg, M. (1979). Temporal duration as a function of information processing. *Perceptual and Motor Skills, 49,* 988–990.

Bjork, R. A. (1978). The updating of human memory. In G. H. Bower (Ed.), *The Psychology of Learning and Motivation* (Vol. 12, pp. 235–259). New York: Academic Press.

Block, R. A. (1974). Memory and the experience of duration in retrospect. *Memory and Cognition, 2,* 153–160.

Block, R. A. (1980). Time and consciousness. In G. Underwood and R. G. Stevens (Eds.), *Aspects of Consciousness* (Vol. 1., pp. 179–217) London: Academic Press.

Block, R. A., George, E. J., and Reed, M. A. (1980). A watched pot sometimes boils: A study of duration experience. *Acta Psychologica, 46,* 81–94.

Brackbill, Y., Fitzgerald, H. E., and Lintz, L. M. (1967). A developmental study of classical conditioning. *Monographs of the Society for Research in Child Development, 32,* Serial No. 116.

Brelsford, J., Jr., Freund, R., and Rundus, D. (1967). Recency judgments in a short-term memory task. *Psychonomic Science, 8,* 247–248.

Brown, A. L. (1973). Judgments of recency for long sequences of pictures: The absence of a developmental trend. *Journal of Experimental Child Psychology, 15,* 473–480.

Brown, N. R., Rips, L. J., and Shevell, S. K. (1985). The subjective dates of natural events in very-long-term memory. *Cognitive Psychology, 17,* 139–177.

Brown, N. R., Shevell, S. K., and Rips, L. J. (1986). Public memories and their personal context. In D. C. Rubin (Ed.), *Autobiographical Memory* (pp. 137–158). Cambridge: Cambridge University Press.

Brown, R., and Kulik, J. (1977). Flashbulb memories. *Cognition, 5,* 73–99.

Brown, S. W. (1985). Time perception and attention: The effects of prospective and retrospective paradigms and task demands on perceived duration. *Perception and Psychophysics, 38,* 115–124.

Brush, E. N. (1930). Observations on the temporal judgment during sleep. *American Journal of Psychology, 42,* 408–411.

Bullock, M., and Gelman, R. (1979). Preschool children's assumptions about cause and effect: Temporal ordering. *Child Development, 50,* 89–96.

Burnam, M. A., Pennebaker, J. W., and Glass, D. C. (1975). Time consciousness, achievement striving, and the type A coronary-prone behavior pattern. *Journal of Abnormal Psychology, 84,* 76–79.

Burnside, W. (1971). Judgment of short time intervals while performing mathematical tasks. *Perception and Psychophysics, 9,* 404–406.

Cahoon, D., and Edmonds, E. M. (1980). The watched pot still won't boil: Expectancy as a variable in estimating the passage of time. *Bulletin of the Psychonomic Society, 16,* 115–116.

Carlson, V. R., Feinberg, I., and Goodenough, D. R. (1978). Perception of the duration of sleep intervals as a function of EEG sleep stage. *Physiological Psychology, 6,* 497–500.

Carni, E., and French, L. A. (1984). The acquisition of before and after reconsidered: What develops? *Journal of Experimental Child Psychology, 37,* 394–403.

Church, R. M. (1984). Properties of the internal clock. In J. Gibbon and L. Allen (Eds.), *Timing and Time Perception* (pp. 566–582). New York: New York Academy of Sciences.

Clark, L. D., Hughes, R., and Nakashima, E. N. (1970). Behavioral effects of marijuana. *Archives of General Psychiatry, 23,* 193–198.

Coate, M. (1964). *Beyond All Reason.* London: Constable.

Collins, A. M., and Loftus, E. F. (1975). A spreading activation theory of semantic processing. *Psychological Review, 82,* 407–428.

Crowder, A. M., and Hohle, R. H. (1970). Time estimation by young children with and without informational feedback. *Journal of Experimental Child Psychology, 10,* 295–307.

Davies, N. B. (1977). Prey selection and the search strategy of the spotted flycatcher (*Musicapa striata*): A field study on optimal foraging. *Animal Behaviour, 25,* 1016–1033.

DeCasper, A. J., and Sigafoos, D. (1983). The intrauterine heartbeat: A potent reinforcer for newborns. *Infant Behavior and Development, 6,* 19–25.

Demany, L., McKenzie, B., and Vurpillot, E. (1977). Rhythm perception in early infancy. *Nature, 266,* 718–719.

Densen, M. E. (1977). Time perception and schizophrenia. *Perceptual and Motor Skills, 44,* 436–438.

De Volder, M. L., and Lens, W. (1982). Academic achievement and future time perspective as a cognitive-motivational concept. *Journal of Personality and Social Psychology, 42,* 566–571.

DeWolfe, R. K. S., and Duncan, C. P. (1959). Time estimation as a function of level of behavior of successive tasks. *Journal of Experimental Psychology, 58,* 153–158.

Dilling, C. A., and Rabin, A. I. (1967). Temporal experience in depressive states and schizophrenia. *Journal of Consulting Psychology, 31,* 604–608.

Edlund, M. (1987). *Psychological Time and Mental Illness.* New York: Gardner Press.

Edmonds, E. M., Cahoon, D., and Bridges, B. (1981). The estimation of time as a function of positive, neutral, or negative expectancies. *Bulletin of the Psychonomic Society, 17,* 259–260.

Eimas, P. D. (1985). The perception of speech in early infancy. *Scientific American, 252,* 46–52.

Eimas, P. D., Siqueland, E. P., Jusczyk, P., and Vigorito, J. (1971). Speech perception in infants. *Science, 171,* 303–306.

Erikson, K. A., and Simon, H. A. (1980). Verbal reports as data. *Psychological Review, 87,* 215–251.

Estes, W. K. (1985). Memory for temporal information. In J. A. Michon and J. Jackson (Eds.), *Time, Mind, and Behavior* (pp. 151–168). Berlin: Springer-Verlag.

Ferguson, R. P., and Martin, P. (1983). Long-term temporal extimation in humans. *Perception and Psychophysics, 33,* 585–592.

Fischer, R. (1966). Biological time. In J. T. Fraser (Ed.), *The Voices of Time* (pp. 357–382). New York: Braziller.

Flexser, A. J., and Bower, G. H. (1974). How frequency affects recency judgments: A model for recency discrimination. *Journal of Experimental Psychology, 103,* 706–716.

Fox, R. H., Bradbury, P. A., Hampton, I. F. G., and Legg, C. F. (1967). Time judgment and body temperature. *Journal of Experimental Psychology, 75,* 88–96.

Fraisse, P. (1963). *The Psychology of Time.* New York: Harper & Row.

Fraisse, P. (1973). Temporal isolation, activity rhythms, and time estimation. In J. L. Rasmussen (Ed.), *Man in Isolation and Confinement* (pp. 85–98). Chicago: Aldine.

Fraisse, P. (1984). Perception and estimation of time. *Annual Review of Psychology,* *35,* 1–36.

Frankenhaeuser, M. (1959). *Estimation of Time: An Experimental Study.* Stockholm: Almqvist & Wiksell.

Freedman, B. J. (1974). The subjective experience of perceptual and cognitive disturbances in schizophrenia. *Archives of General Psychiatry, 30,* 333–340.

French, L. A., and Nelson, K. (1981). Temporal knowledge expressed in preschoolers' descriptions of familiar activities. *Papers and Reports on Child Language Development, 20,* 61–69.

Friedman, A. S. (1964). Minimal effects of severe depression on cognitive functioning. *Journal of Abnormal and Social Psychology, 69,* 237–243.

Friedman, E. R. (1977). Judgment of time intervals by young children. *Perceptual and Motor Skills, 45,* 715–720.

Friedman, W. J. (1977). The development of children's knowledge of cyclic aspects of time. *Child Development, 48,* 1593–1599.

Friedman, W. J. (1978). Development of time concepts in children. In H. W. Reese and L. P. Lipsitt (Eds.), *Advances in Child Development and Behavior, 12,* 267–298. New York: Academic Press.

Friedman, W. J. (1982). Conventional time concepts and children's structuring of time. In W. J. Friedman (Ed.), *The Developmental Psychology of Time* (pp. 171–208). New York: Academic Press.

Friedman, W. J. (1983). Image and verbal processes in reasoning about the months of the year. *Journal of Experimental Psychology: Learning, Memory, and Cognition, 9,* 650–666.

Friedman, W. J. (1984). Analog and semantic models of judgments about the months of the year. *Memory and Cognition, 12,* 306–313.

Friedman, W. J. (1986). The development of children's knowledge of temporal structure. *Child Developppment, 57,* 1386–1400.

Friedman, W. J. (1987). A follow-up to "Scale effects in memory for the time of events": The earthquake study. *Memory and Cognition, 15,* 518–520.

Friedman, W. J. (1989). The representation of temporal structure in children, adolescents and adults. In I. Levin and D. Zakay (Eds.), *Psychological Time: A Life Span Perspective* (pp. 259–304). Amsterdam: North-Holland.

Friedman, W. J. (in press). Children's representations of the pattern of daily activities. *Child Development.*

Friedman, W. J., and Seeley, P. B. (1976). The child's acquisition of spatial and temporal word meanings. *Child Development, 47,* 1103–1108.

Friedman, W. J., and Wilkins, A. J. (1985). Scale effects in memory for the time of events. *Memory and Cognition, 13,* 168–175.

Fuhrman, R. W., and Wyer, R. S., Jr. (1988). Event memory: Temporal order judgments of personal life experiences. *Journal of Personality and Social Psychology, 54,* 365–384.

Gallistel, C. R. (1989). *The Organization of Learning.* Cambridge, MA: MIT Press.

Galton, F. (1880). Visualized numerals. *Nature, 21,* 252–256.

Galton, F. (1883). *Inquiries into Human Faculty and Its Development.* London: Macmillan.

Gastorf, J. W. (1980). Time urgency of the type A behavior pattern. *Journal of Consulting and Clinical Psychology, 48,* 299.

Glazier, J. (1976). Generation classes among the Mbeere of central Kenya. *Africa, 46,* 313–325.

Glenberg, A. M., and Swanson, N. G. (1986). A temporal distinctiveness theory of recency and modality effects. *Journal of Experimental Psychology: Learning, Memory, and Cognition, 12,* 3–15.

Godden, D. R., and Baddeley, A. D. (1975). Context-dependent memory in two natural environments: On land and under water. *British Journal of Psychology, 66,* 325–331.

Goldstone, S., Boardman, W. K., and Lhamon, W. T. (1958). Effect of quinal barbitone, dextro-amphetamine, and placebo on apparent time. *British Journal of Psychology, 49,* 324–328.

Goldstone, S., and Kirkham, J. E. (1968). The effects of secobarbital and dextroamphetamine upon time judgment: Intersensory factors. *Psychopharmacologia, 13,* 65–73.

Goldstone, S., and Lhamon, W. T. (1976). Signal pulse-rate and judged duration. *Perceptual and Motor Skills, 42,* 655–661.

Goleman, D. (1986). Perception of time emerges as key psychological factor. *The New York Times,* 30 December, 15–16.

Gonzales, A., and Zimbardo, P. G. (1985). Time in perspective. *Psychology Today, 19,* 21–26.

Green, T. R. G., and Simpson, A. J. (1977). Time and temperature: A note on Bell. *Quarterly Journal of Experimental Psychology, 29,* 337–340.

Guenther, R. K., and Linton, M. (1975). Mechanisms of temporal coding. *Journal of Experimental Psychology: Human Learning and Memory, 97,* 220–229.

Guilford, J. P. (1926). Spatial symbols in the apprehension of time. *American Journal of Psychology, 37,* 420–423.

Guyau, J. M. (1890). *La Genèse de l'Idée de Temps.* Paris: Alcan.

Haake, R. J., and Somerville, S. C. (1985). Development of logical search skills in infancy. *Developmental Psychology, 21,* 176–186.

Hadamard, J. (1945). *An Essay on the Psychology of Invention in the Mathematical Field.* Princeton: Princeton University Press.

Hallowell, I. (1937). Temporal orientation in western civilization and in a pre-literate society. *American Anthropologist, 39,* 647–670.

Hamilton, J. M. E., and Sanford, A. J. (1978). The symbolic distance effect for alphabetic order judgments: A subjective report and reaction time analysis. *Quarterly Journal of Experimental Psychology, 30,* 33–43.

Hancock, P. A. (1984). An endogenous metric for the control of brief temporal intervals. In J. Gibbon and L. Allen (Eds.), *Timing and Time Perception* (pp. 594–596). New York: New York Academy of Sciences.

Harner, L. (1981). Children talk about the time and aspect of actions. *Child Development, 52,* 498–506.

Harner, L. (1982). Talking about the past and future. In W. J. Friedman (Ed.), *The Developmental Psychology of Time* (pp. 141–169). New York: Academic Press.

Hawkins, M. F., and Tedford, W. H., Jr. (1976). Effects of interest and relatedness on estimated duration of verbal material. *Bulletin of the Psychonomic Society, 8,* 301–302.

Hawkins, W. L., French, L. C., Crawford, B. D., and Enzle, M. E. (1988). Depressed affect and time perception. *Journal of Abnormal Psychology, 97,* 275–280.

Hicks, R. E., Gualtieri, C. T., Mayo, J. P., Jr., and Perez-Reyes, M. (1984). Cannabis, atropine and temporal information processing. *Neuropsychobiology, 12,* 229–237.

Hicks, R. E., Miller, G. W., Gaes, G., and Bierman, K. (1977). Concurrent processing demands and the experience of time in passing. *American Journal of Psychology, 90,* 431–446.

Hicks, R. E., Miller, G. W., and Kinsbourne, M. (1976). Prospective and retrospective judgments of time as a function of amount of information presented. *American Journal of Psychology, 89,* 719–730.

Hinrichs, J. V., and Buschke, H. (1968). Judgment of recency under steady-state conditions. *Journal of Experimental Psychology, 78,* 574–579.

Hintzman, D. L., and Block, R. A. (1971). Repetition and memory: Evidence for a multiple trace hypothesis. *Journal of Experimental Psychology, 88, 297–306.*

Hintzman, D. L., Block, R. A., and Summers, J. J. (1973). Contextual associations and memory for serial position. *Journal of Experimental Psychology, 97,* 220–229.

Hintzman, D. L., Summers, J. J., and Block, R. A. (1975). Spacing judgments as an index of study-phase retrieval. *Journal of Experimental Psychology: Human Learning and Memory, 1,* 31–40.

Hoagland, H. (1966). Some biochemical considerations of time. In J. T. Fraser (Ed.), *The Voices of Time* (pp. 312–329). New York: Braziller.

Howe, L. E. A. (1981). The social determination of knowledge: Maurice Bloch and Balinese time. *Man, 16,* 220–234.

Hurst, W., and Volpe, B. T. (1982). Temporal order judgements with amnesia. *Brain and Cognition, 1,* 294–306.

James, W. (1890). *The Principles of Psychology* (Vol. 1). New York: Henry Holt & Co.

Joubert, C. E. (1983). Subjective acceration of time: Death anxiety and sex differences. *Perceptual and Motor Skills, 57,* 49–50.

Joubert, C. E. (1984). Structured time and subjective acceration of time. *Perceptual and Motor Skills, 59,* 335–336.

Klahr, D., Chase, W. G., and Lovelace, E. A. (1983). Structure and process in alphabetic retrieval. *Journal of Experimental Psychology: Learing, Memory, and Cognition, 9,* 462–477.

Koffka, K. (1935). *Principles of Gestalt Psychology.* New York: Harcourt, Brace & World

Koriat, A., and Fischhoff, B. (1974). What day is today? An inquiry into the process of time orientation. *Memory and Cognition, 2,* 201–205.

Koriat, A., Fischhoff, B., and Razel, O. (1976). An inquiry into the process of temporal orientation. *Acta Psychologica, 40,* 57–73.

Kosslyn, S. M., and Pomerantz, J. R. (1977). Imagery, propositions, and the form of internal representations. *Cognitive Psychology, 9,* 52–76.

Krebs, J. R., and Kacelnik, A. (1984). Time horizons and foraging animals. In J. Gibbon and L. Allen (Eds.), *Timing and Time Perception* (pp. 278–291). New York: New York Academy of Sciences.

Kuipers, B. (1978). Modeling spatial knowledge. *Cognitive Science, 2,* 129–153.

Langer, J., Wapner, S., and Wener, H. (1961). The effect of danger upon the experience of time. *American Journal of Psychology, 74,* 94–97.

Lea, S. E. G., and Dow, S. M. (1984). Integration of reinforcements over time. In J. Gibbon and L. Allen (Eds.), *Timing and Time Perception* (pp. 269–277). New York: New York Academy of Sciences.

Lemlich, R. (1975). Subjective acceleration of time with aging. *Perceptual and Motor Skills, 41,* 235–238.

Levin, I. (1977). The development of time concepts in young children: Reasoning about duration. *Child Development, 48,* 435–444.

Levin, I. (1982). The nature and development of time concepts in children: The effects of interfering cues. In W. J. Friedman (Ed.), *The Developmental Pshchology of Time* (pp. 47–85). New York: Academic Press.

Levine, R., and Wolff, E. (1985). Social time: The heartbeat of culture. *Psychology Today, 19*, 29–35.

Levine, R. V., West, L. J., and Reis, H. T. (1980). Perception of time and punctuality in the United States and Brazil. *Journal of Personality and Social Psychology, 38*, 541–550.

Lewkowicz, D. J. (1985). Developmental changes in infants' response to temporal frequency. *Developmental Psychology, 21*, 858–865.

Lewkowicz, D. J. (1989). The role of temporal factors in infant behavior and development. In I. Levin and D. Zakay (Eds.), *Time and Human Cognition: A Life-Span Perspective* (pp. 9–62). Amsterdam: North-Holland.

Lieury, A., Aiello, B., Lepreux, D., and Mellet, M. (1980). Le role de reperes dans la recuperation et la datation des souvenirs. *Année Psychologique, 80*, 149–167.

Lieury, A., Caplain, P., Jacquet, A., and Jolivet, C. (1979). La contraction du temps dans la datation des souvenirs anciens. *Année Psychologique, 79*, 7–22.

Linton, M. (1975). Memory for real world events. In D. A. Norman and D. E. Rumelhart (Eds.), *Explorations in Cognition*. San Francisco: Freeman.

Lowin, A., Hottes, J. H., Sandler, B. E., and Bornstein, M. (1971). The pace of life and sensitivity to time in urban and rural settings. *Journal of Social Psychology, 83*, 247–253.

Lovelace, E. A., Powell, C. M., and Brooks, R. J. (1973). Alphabetic position effects in covert and overt alphabetic recitation times. *Journal of Experimental Psychology, 99*, 405–408.

Macar, F. (1980). *Le Temps: Perspectives Psychophysiologiques*. Brussels: Mardaga.

Macar, F. (1988). Temporal regulation in children 3 to 5 years old. *Cahiers de Psychologie Cognitive, 8*, 39–51.

Macar, F., and Grondin, S. (1988). Temporal regulation as a function of muscular parameters in 5-year-old children. *Journal of Experimental Child Psychology, 45*, 159–174.

McClain, L. (1983). Interval estimation: Effects of processing demands on prospective and retrospective reports. *Perception and Psychophysics, 34*, 185–189.

Mandler, J. M., Seegmiller, D., and Day, J. (1977). On the coding of spatial information. *Memory and Cognition, 5*, 10–16.

Martin, G. A., Shumate, M., and Frauenfelder, K. (1981). Experience of duration as a function of number of responses, task difficulty, and sex. *Perceptual and Motor Skills, 53*, 139–145.

Mathews, M. E., and Fozard, J. L. (1970). Age differences in judgments of recency for short sequences of pictures. *Developmental Psychology, 3*, 208–217.

Meck, W. H., and Church, R. M. (1984). Simultaneous temporal processing. *Journal of Experimental Psychology: Animal Behavior Processes, 10*, 1–29.

Melges, F. T. (1982). *Time and the Inner Future: A Temporal Approach to Psychiatric Disorders*. New York: Wiley.

Melges, F. T. (1988). Guyau on the illusions of time: Normal and pathological. In J. A. Michon, V. Pouthas, and J. Jackson (Eds.), *Guyau and the Idea of Time* (pp. 213–231). Amsterdam: North-Holland.

Melges, F. T., and Fougerousse, C. E. (1966). Time sense, emotions, and acute mental illness. *Journal of Psychiatric Research, 4*, 127–140.

Mezey, A. G., and Cohen, S. I. (1961). The effect of depressive illness on time judgment and time experience. *Journal of Neurology, Neurosurgery and Psychiatry, 24*, 269–270.

Michon, J. A. (1965). Studies on subjective duration: II. Subjective time measurement during tasks with different information content. *Acta Psychologica, 24,* 205–219.

Michon, J. A., Pouthas, V., and Jackson, J. (Eds.) (1988). *Guyau and the Idea of Time.* Amsterdam: North-Holland.

Miller, G. A., and Johnson-Laird, P. N. (1976). *Language and Perception.* Cambridge, MA: Harvard University Press.

Miller, G. W., Hicks, R. E., and Willette, M. (1978). Effects of concurrent verbal rehearsal and temporal set upon judgments of temporal duration. *Acta Psychologica, 42,* 173–179.

Milner, B., Corkin, S., and Teuber, H.-L. (1968). Further analysis of the hippocampal amnesic syndrome: A 14-year follow-up study of H. M. *Neuropsychologia, 6,* 215–235.

Montangero, J. (1985). The development of temporal inferences and meanings in 5- to 8-year-old children. In J. A. Michon and J. L. Jackson (Eds.), *Time, Mind, and Behavior* (pp. 279–287). Berlin: Springer-Verlag.

Moore-Ede, M. C., Sulzman, F. M., and Fuller, C. A. (1982). *The Clocks that Time Us; Physiology of the Circadian Timing System.* Cambridge, MA: Harvard University Press.

Morrongiello, B. A. (1984). Auditory temporal pattern perception in 6- and 12-month-old infants. *Developmental Psychology, 20,* 441–448.

Morrongiello, B. A., and Trehub, S. E. (1987). Age-related changes in auditory temporal perception. *Journal of Experimental Child Psychology, 44,* 413–426.

Morton, J. (1968). Repeated items and decay in memory. *Psychonomic Science, 10,* 219–220.

Mulligan, R. M., and Schiffman, H. R. (1979). Temporal experience as a function of organization in memory. *Bulletin of the Psychonomic Society, 14,* 417–420.

Murdock, B. B., Jr. (1974). *Human Memory: Theory and Data.* Potomac, MD: Erlbaum.

Muto, T. (1982). [The structure of "life-time" in young children.] *Japanese Journal of Educational Psychology, 30,* 185–191.

Nelson, K. (1978). How children represent knowledge of their world in and out of language: A preliminary report. In R. Siegler (Ed.), *Children's Thinking: What Develops?* (pp. 255–273). Hillsdale, NJ: Erlbaum.

Nelson, K. (1986). *Event Knowledge, Structure and Function in Development.* Hillsdale, NJ: Erlbaum.

Nelson, K., and Gruendel, J. (1981). Generalized event representations: Basic building blocks of cognitive development. In M. E. Lamb and A. L. Brown (Eds.), *Advances in Developmental Psychology* (Vol. 1, pp. 131–158). Hillsdale, NJ: Erlbaum.

Newman, M. A., and Gaudiano, J. K. (1984). Depression as an explanation for decreased subjective time in the elderly. *Nursing Research, 33,* 137–139.

Noble, W. G., and Lundie, R. E. (1974). Temporal discrimination of short intervals of dreamless sleep. *Perceptual and Motor Skills, 38,* 445–446.

O'Connell, B. G., and Gerard, A. B. (1985). Scripts and scraps: The development of sequential understanding. *Child Development, 56,* 671–681.

Ohnuki-Tierney, E. (1973). Sakhalin Ainu time reckoning. *Man, 8,* 285–299.

Ornstein, R. E. (1969). *On the Experience of Time.* Harmondsworth, England: Penguin.

Osgood, C. E., May, W. H., and Miron, M. S. (1975). *Cross-Cultural Universals of Affective Meaning.* Urbana: University of Illinois Press.

Oswald, I. (1960). Number-forms and kindred visual images. *Journal of General Psychology, 63,* 81–88.

Paivio, A. (1971). *Imagery and Verbal Processes*. New York: Holt, Rinehart & Winston.

Paivio, A. (1978). Comparisons of mental clocks. *Journal of Experimental Psychology: Human Perception and Performance, 4*, 61–71.

Paivio, A. (1986). *Mental Representations; A Dual Coding Approach*. New York: Oxford University Press.

Pavlov, I. (1960). *Conditioned Reflexes*. New York: Dover.

Peterson, L. R., Johnson, S. T., and Coatney, R. (1969). The effect of repeated oc-curences on judgments of recency. *Journal of Verbal Learning and Verbal Behavior, 8*, 591–596.

Piaget, J. (1952). *The Origins of Intelligence in Children*. New York: International Uni-versities Press.

Piaget, J. (1954). *The Construction of Reality in the Child*. New York: Basic Books.

Piaget, J. (1969). *The Child's Conception of Time*. London: Routledge & Kegan Paul.

Pillemer, D. B. (1984). Flashbulb memories of the assassination attempt on President Reagan. *Cognition, 16*, 63–80.

Pouthas, V. (1985). Timing behavior in young children: A developmental approach to conditioned spaced responding. In J. A. Michon and J. L. Jackson (Eds.), *Time, Mind, and Behavior* (pp. 100–109). Berlin: Springer-Verlag.

Pouthas, V., and Jacquet, A. Y. (1987). A developmental study of timing behavior in 4½- and 7-year-old children. *Journal of Experimental Child Psychology, 43*, 282–299.

Poynter, W. D. (1983). Duration judgment and the segmentation of experience. *Memory and Cognition, 11*, 77–82.

Poynter, W. D. (1989). Judging the duration of intervals: A process of remembering segments of experience. In I. Levin and D. Zakay (Eds.), *Psychological Time: A Lifespan Perspective* (pp. 305–331). Amsterdam: North-Holland.

Predebon, J. (1984). Organization of stimulus events and remembered apparent du-ration. *Australian Journal of Psychology, 36*, 161–169.

Quigley, J. J., Combs, A. L., and O'Leary, N. (1984). Sensed duration of time: Influ-ence of time as a barrier. *Perceptual and Motor Skills, 58*, 72–74.

Rappaport, H., Enrich, K., and Wilson, A. (1985). Relation between ego identity and temporal perspective. *Journal of Personality and Social Psychology, 48*, 1609–1620.

Retzlaff, P. D. (1982). Verbal estimation, production, and reproduction of time in-tervals by type A individuals. *Perceptual and Motor Skills, 55*, 331–334.

Ribot, T. (1901) *Les Maladies de la Mémoire*. Paris: Alcan.

Richards, W. (1973). Time reproductions by H. M. *Acta Psychologica, 37*, 279-282.

Richelle, M., and Lejeune, H. (Eds.) (1980). *Time in Animal Behavior*. New York: Pergamon.

Roberts, S. (1983). Properties and function of an internal clock. In R. L. Mellgren (Ed.), *Animal Cognition and Behavior* (pp. 345–397). Amsterdam: North Holland.

Robinson, J. A. (1986). Temporal reference systems and autobiographical memory. In D. C. Rubin (Ed.), *Autobiographical Memory*. Cambridge: Cambridge Univer-sity Press.

Rothkopf, E. Z. (1971). Incidental memory for location of information in text. *Journal of Verbal Learning and Verbal Behavior, 10*, 608–613.

Sacks, O. (1985). *The Man Who Mistook His Wife for a Hat*. London: Duckworth.

Sanders, H. I., and Warrington, E. K. (1971). Memory for remote events in amnesic patients. *Brain, 94*, 661–668.

Schulman, A. I. (1973). Recognition, memory, and the coding of spatial location. *Memory and Cognition, 1*, 256–260.

Schroeder, J. E. (1980). Imaginary representation of time cycles. *Perceptual and Motor Skills, 50,* 723–734.

Seymour, P. H. K. (1980a). Internal representation of the months; An experimental analysis of spatial forms. *Psychological Research, 42,* 255–273.

Seymour, P. H. K. (1980b). Semantic and structural coding of the months. *British Journal of Psychology, 71,* 379–393.

Shaffer, L. H. (1985). Timing in action. In J. A. Michon and J. L. Jackson (Eds.), *Time, Mind, and Behavior* (pp. 226–241). Berlin: Springer-Verlag.

Shanon, B. (1979). Yesterday, today and tomorrow. *Acta Psychologica, 43,* 469–476.

Shepard, R. N. (1978). Externalization of mental images and the act of creation. In B. S. Randhawa and W. E. Coffman (Eds.), *Visual Learning, Thinking and Communication.* New York: Academic Press.

Shepard, R. N., and Podgorny, P. (1978). Cognitive processes that resemble perceptual processes. In W. Estes (Ed.), *Handbook of Learning and Cognitive Processes, Volume 5, Human Information Processing* (pp. 189–237). Hillsdale, NJ: Erlbaum.

Siegler, R. S., and Richards, D. D. (1979). Development of time, speed, and distance concepts. *Developmental Psychology, 15,* 288–298.

Silver, R., and Bittman, E. L. (1984). Reproductive mechanisms: Interaction of circadian and interval timing. In J. Gibbon and L. Allen (Eds.), *Timing and Time Perception* (pp. 488–514). New York: New York Academy of Sciences.

Skinner, B. F. (1956). A case history in the scientific method. *American Psychologist, 2,* 221–233.

Smith, N. C. (1969). The effect on time estimation of increasing the complexity of a cognitive task. *Journal of General Psychology, 81,* 231–235.

Smith, S. M. (1979). Remembering in and out of context. *Journal of Experimental Psychology: Human Learning and Memory, 5,* 342–361.

Squire, L. R. (1982). Comparisons between forms of amnesia: Some deficits are unique to Korsakoff's syndrome. *Journal of Experimental Psychology: Learning, Memory, and Cognition, 8,* 560–571.

Squire, L. R. (1987). *Memory and Brain.* New York: Oxford University Press.

Squire, L. R., Chase, P. M., and Slater, P. C. (1975). Assessment of memory for remote events. *Psychological Reports, 37,* 223–234.

Squire, L. R., Nadel, L., and Slater, P. C. (1981). Anterograde amnesia and memory for temporal order. *Neuropsychologia, 19,* 141–145.

Stevenson, R. J., and Pollitt, C. (1987). The acquisition of temporal terms. *Journal of Child Language, 14,* 533–545.

Tebecis, A. K., and Provins, K. A. (1974). Accuracy of time estimation during hypnosis. *Perceptual and Motor Skills, 39,* 1123–1126.

Thomas, E. A. C., and Weaver, W. B. (1975). Cognitive processing and time perception. *Perception and Psychophysics, 17,* 363–367.

Thompson, C. P. (1982). Memory for unique personal events: The roommate study. *Memory and Cognition, 10,* 324–332.

Tinklenberg, J. R., Roth, W. T., and Koppell, B. S. (1976). Marijuana and ethanol: Differential effects on time perception, heart rate, and subjective response. *Psychopharmacology, 49,* 275–279.

Toglia, M. P., and Kimble, G. A. (1976). Recall and use of serial position information. *Journal of Experimental Psychology: Human Learning and Memory, 2,* 431–445.

Treisman, M. (1963). Temporal discrimination and the indifference interval: Implications for a model of the "internal clock." *Psychological Monographs: General and Applied, 77,* No. 13, Whole No. 576, 1–13.

Tulving, E. (1985a). How many memory systems are there? *American Psychologist, 40,* 385–398.

Tulving, E. (1985b). Memory and consciousness. *Canadian Psychology, 26,* 1–12.

Turton, D., and Ruggles, C. (1978). Agreeing to disagree: The measurement of duration in a southwestern Ethiopian community. *Current Anthropology, 19,* 585–600.

Tysk, L. (1983). Estimation of time and the subclassification of schizophrenic disorders. *Perceptual and Motor Skills, 57,* 911–918.

Tysk, L. (1984a). Time perception and affective disorders. *Perceptual and Motor Skills, 58,* 455–464.

Tysk, L. (1984b). A longitudinal study of time estimation in psychotic disorders. *Perceptual and Motor Skills, 59,* 779–789.

Tysk, L. (1985). Longitudinal changes in time estimation in affective disorders: A preliminary study. *Perceptual and Motor Skills, 60,* 179–188.

Tzeng, O. J. L. (1976). A precedence effect in the processing of verbal information. *American Journal of Psychology, 89,* 577–599.

Tzeng, O. J. L., and Cotton, B. (1980). A study-phase retrieval model of temporal coding. *Journal of Experimental Psychology: Human Learning and Memory, 6,* 705–716.

Tzeng, O. J. L., Lee, A. T., and Wetzel, C. D. (1979). Temporal coding in verbal information processing. *Journal of Experimental Psychology: Human Learning and Memory, 5,* 52–64.

Underwood, B. J. (1977). *Temporal Codes for Memories: Issues and Problems.* Hillsdale, NJ: Erlbaum.

Underwood, G. (1975). Attention and the perception of duration during encoding and retrieval. *Perception, 4,* 291–296.

Underwood, G., and Swain, R. A. (1973). Selectivity of attention and the perception of duration. *Perception, 2,* 101–105.

van Benthem, J. (1985). Semantics of time. In J. A. Michon and J. L. Jackson (Eds.), *Time, Mind, and Behavior* (pp. 266–278). Berlin: Springer-Verlag.

von Wright, J. M. (1973). Judgment of relative recency: Developmental trends. *The Journal of Psychology, 84,* 3–12.

Vroon, P. A. (1970). Effects of presented and processed information on duration experience. *Acta Psychologica, 34,* 115–121.

Wagenaar, W. A. (1986). My memory: A study of autobiographical memory over six years. *Cognitive Psychology, 18,* 225–252.

Wahl, O. F., and Seig, D. (1980). Time estimation among schizophrenics. *Perceptual and Motor Skills, 50,* 535–541.

Walker, J. L. (1977). Time estimation and total subjective time. *Perceptual and Motor Skills, 44,* 527–532.

Weist, R. M. (1989). Time concepts in language and thought: Filling the Piagetian void from two to five years. In I. Levin and D. Zakay (Eds.), *Time and Human Cognition: A Lifespan Perspective* (pp. 63–118). Amsterdam: North-Holland.

Weist, R. M., Wysocka, H., Witkowska-Stadnik, K., Buczowska, E., and Konieczna, E. (1984). The defective tense hypothesis: on the emergence of tense and aspect in child Polish. *Journal of Child Language, 11,* 347–374.

Wells, J. E. (1974). Strength theory and judgments of recency and frequency. *Journal of Verbal Learning and Behavior, 13,* 378–392.

Werner, H., and Kaplan, B. (1963). *Symbol Formation.* New York: Wiley.

Wilkening, F., Levin, I., and Druyan, S. (1987). Children's counting strategies for time quantification and integration. *Developmental Psychology, 23,* 823–831.

Wilsoncroft, W. E., and Stone, J. D. (1975). Information processing and estimation of short time intervals. *Perceptual and Motor Skills, 41,* 192–194.

Winograd, E., and Solloway, R. M. (1985). Reminding as a basis for temporal judgments. *Journal of Experimental Psychology: Learning, Memory, and Cognition, 11,* 262–271.

Wright, L. (1988). The type A behavior pattern and coronary artery disease: Quest for the active ingredients and the elusive mechanism. *American Psychologist, 43,* 2–14.

Wyrick, R. A., and Wyrick, L. C. (1977). Time experience during depression. *Archives of General Psychiatry, 34,* 1441–1443.

Yarnold, P. R., and Grimm, L. G. (1982). Time urgency among coronary-prone individuals. *Journal of Abnormal Psychology, 91,* 175–177.

Yntema, D. B., and Trask, F. P. (1963). Recall as a search process. *Journal of Verbal Learning and Verbal Behavior, 2,* 65–74.

Zakay, D. (1989). Subjective time and attentional resource allocation: An integrated model of time estimation. In I. Levin and D. Zakay (Eds.), *Psychological Time: A Lifespan Perspective* (pp. 365–397). Amsterdam: North Holland.

Zakay, D., and Fallach, E. (1984). Immediate and remote time estimation—A comparison. *Acta Psychologica, 57,* 69–81.

Zakay, D., Nitzan, D., and Glicksohn, J. (1983). The influence of task difficulty and external tempo on subjective time estimation. *Perception and Psychophysics, 34,* 451–456.

Zerubavel, E. (1981). *Hidden Rhythms: Schedules and Calendars in Social Life.* Chicago: The University of Chicago Press.

Zerubavel, E. (1985). *The Seven Day Circle.* New York: The Free Press.

Zimbardo, P. G., and Gonzales, A. (1984). The times of your life. *Psychology Today, 18,* 53–54.

Index